A list of your author's books

are attached in the back of this book

for your inspection.

Preventing the Doom of Mankind

A Realistic and Factual Approach
of what is forming

Lloyd E. McIlveen

 www.trafford.com

North America & international
toll-free: 1 888 232 4444 (USA & Canada)
fax: 812 355 4082

This is an introduction to life or death of humanity

Everything may appear to be functioning fairly normal in our everyday progressing routines of work, family life, eating, drinking, constant traffic and the never ending struggle to acquire money, fame, glory, a career, love or other seeming necessities of life including having to exercise dominant natures and normal addictions or anything that makes us feel good. We as a human species live in the spoils of plenty and maybe, unfortunately, more to come.

However, we humans of the twenty-first century are living in a very tumultuously critical and wildly dangerous time for surviving and getting along with each other. We need a reasonable and objecting change in how we perceive and approach our relationships with our world of intelligence, ignorance, people and our world itself if we have any belief or expectations of our future to continue.

That assumed and expected continuance of living beings on planet Earth is now at risk of succumbing and yielding to the developing forces of mankind's contributions to their progress over the lifetime of their civilized existence.

Many phases of human progress have exacerbated the chances for the species to universally exist in a forever type system of planets and stars.

These scripts offer a possibility for a newly developed opportunity to rearrange the destiny of mankind for living into that forever type scene as time passes.

The descriptions of how all living beings will vanish from the globe sooner than later will be mentioned repeatedly throughout this book so it rings home solidly as not only very important issues, but also as meaningful consciousness needed by our people of the world in this time of human existence, that is, if the majority of the world's people want the human and animal species to survive this approaching cataclysmic temperature change of which mankind has caused. The more we become aware of how we have caused it, the more we can handle offsetting that dilemma with the world cooperation of one another. Also, you will notice one issue is particularly repeated twice as a benefit in different contexts of what I, your author, feel is significant and analogous information that may add toward the readers evaluation of this subject.

Good luck with your patience in acknowledging our dilemma and possibilities for survival via the introduction, preface and following chapters on one of "the" most important issues of our time.

Preface

Most of us are a bit or more anxious about getting something accomplished large or small or even getting to a point of not having to do anything.

Obviously and even when all seems somewhat quiet with all the hustle and bustle of people's societies, the tension of wishing, hoping, waiting or gun jumping to acquire something before someone else does has been driving us all into a dog eat dog type syndrome that makes one wonder what all this is leading to. Is this the destined course of our future? Back in the so-called "good old days" when progress, money, politics or other chaos became intensified, it was somewhere else in the world. Now it's everywhere on the globe and no one seems to know how to get it back on track of normalcy, whatever that may be.

Many appearances seem, presently, we are headed into an unscrupulous, detrimental and irreversible period of human deterioration where everyone perishes from the face of the earth. It may be true. That's the way it appears from hords of people and their calculated views where no one can trust anyone any more and it can only get worse.

However, that's fairly normal when growth consensus moves forward in its analysis faster than new changes in societies of the world can rationally and practically absorb, tolerate and disperse in their many directions of those societies. Many of those glittering and deceiving changes appear on the surface to be widely needed for creating and maintaining our societal and family balance, but that may be an erroneous conjecture of which must be reevaluated in a humble and perspective manner for saving the world's people from massive ruination and inevitable termination. Most roads of direction display signs of an eventual dead end of life; all of ours do to the unwillingness of most everyone to change their insufficient views on survival.

The following chapters are designed and displayed to present workable solutions of which could, can or better; "will" set us all on a destined course for a journey of survival into our future. Of course, that's for all of us who desire to be serious in these efforts, not for freeloaders who just want a free ride into our worthwhile future with no belief or support to it unless they want to change too.

The chapters are written with gusto to inspire a cause for everyone's participation in promoting reason to get involved in this way overdue encounter in developing what we all have been looking forward to; a better world of people than we were. We need that kind of growth for vibrant survival.

We "are" becoming more intelligent. Even though intelligence has had its share of stumbling as it has in the stock market. The market has always come back up and went further forward. Intelligence will always prevail. That's what this book is about; rebounding, even in the darkest time of doubt. It's about our past, present and future destinations which are starkly unembellished with realistic estimates and contentions of how our future will unfold. The scripts are loaded with many mentioned reminders where mankind has led us into a destiny of doom if we hesitate too long in correcting our errors. Creative guidance is displayed to offset that doom. This is literature of reality in the raw.

Contents

Chapter 1

Our present world predicaments started way back when

People never were very good at organizing efficiently for whatever cause they thought was necessary. History way back to the stone age and prior to that has proven it. Early mankind was famous for lazy habits of only tending to the moment's needs such as securing a roof, food, sleep, sex and defensive measures to some degree.

Whoever thought, in those earlier times of biological development, their entire environments would come tumbling down on all of them in so many different ways because of their inappropriate habits of not preparing for humanistically created disasters, failures, errors greed and a long list of surmounting problems of which "did" begin with "their" indolent mannerisms.

The habits of putting strategic planning off to a later time has had a profound effect of becoming an inherited detriment to an improved quality of life of which we "could" have had up to now. However, they didn't prepare for the future benefits of now. Obviously, there was a lack of guidance influencing mankind to prepare better for a smooth flow of human progress into the future. Religious belief wasn't enough as profoundly influencial as it was. More responsible efforts of the people was needed.

Now, in this day of our questionable future, we have some work to do in developing our abilities to prepare our families of humans for a more gracious, peaceful and stable future. Too bad it took so long to see what happened to correct it.

The beginning and continued past of our procreated entry into this life is totally necessary to understand for the benefit of preventing repeat performances of that past which were:

1. Early man didn't have insight in each of the human families, groups or clans for future survival because of not being inherent like wolves and other animals.

2. Mankind, throughout their early struggles of day to day existence for eons of time had little or no confidence to insightly handle imaginative or speculative concepts of what may unfold with worldly functions let alone the vast progress of humanity we now retrospectively view.

3. There is very little prehistoric evidence supporting any "divine" or other spiritual type guidance for gaining the confidence needed in expanding their worldly or local progress of civilization which matured slowly only to turn into a nightmare later.

4. Without worldly consciousness of some kind, early man was more primarily involved in

protecting themselves from intruders who wanted what they had. Through efforts of "all" their ignorances, both sides instinctively devised weapons to protect themselves or kill the offenders; hence war began and seemingly has been quite dependable and popular in continuing for solving most discrepancies of ownership and/or principle etc. Most people have always agreed war hasn't been wanted even though those methods have been very conventional and apparently needed from habitual or proven encounters over time. The propagators of those encounters haven't changed much.

5. Most failures in history have been due to poor planning and that goes "way" back. Poor planning usually occurred because of not considering enough importance for what the inevitable and ongoing results would be.

6. Results of past failures were only strived for at the time the promoters were living and usually

strived for individual or power inspired desires. That never achieved world compatibility and has been proven to be only a culturally driven desire of habit inflicted by so many humans. Even our predecessor animals of whom we have believed to be so much less intelligent than us rarely suffered extensive failures as mankind has. They were here a lot longer than we ever were and flowed along easily through the very long course of earthly existence for millions of years if not longer. They were no threat to their extinction. Why have "we" become the culprits? Let's move along and discover.

7. One of the biggest ongoing mistakes mankind ever made, whether it was only a few in earlier times or massive amounts in more recent times, was only caring about their own families or their own cause without consideration of how humans would eventually become massively affiliated somehow like ants, birds, fish and zebra for

instance as we are today. This poor planning is still a big factor in the present predicaments on Earth and it all started so long ago. It isn't the fault of any leaders particularly. It's everyone's fault. We are now beginning to see it here and there, but it's not enough for the people of the world to understand for making changes yet. When they do get it, it may be too late. We have to help them through efforts of which we are engaging in from this book forward. Making changes is critical now.

8. Mankind acquired abilities over eons of time to teach subjects dealing with everyday necessities as knowledge for some surviving, but mostly for learning about art, communicable skills and languages for exchanging products and services which eventually became sources of gaining power over others; not necessarily a combined power for creating a better world of people. It hasn't changed much yet. It has habitually and

timely became a way of life mostly for the time being. It is more currently described as the "now" with more emphasis on getting what one wants only while living on this planet and less regard for anyone in the future. Improving our present attitudes on the value of humanity will influence the survival of our present and future generations. Past and future is the essence of importance in determining what to and how to solve and resolve world predicaments. The past is there for reference and the future is to be conscientiously or haphazardly delt with. We can take our pick. The interim (the "now") does not exist because the now becomes the past as soon as it is said. Reviewing our perception on time will help our survival.

There are, of course, many books and films etc. on mankind's past in endless respect. This chapter briefly describes some general ideas of how man's momentarily developed and continuously practiced habits were passed down through the ages that largely contributed to present world chaos and predicamental conditions of which we now have to shift around for a more pleasant world of people. We need to start becoming much more conscious of what we have promoted from millenniums of time back in our earlier development up to this present era time with the exception of the Dark Ages and more recent setbacks as the bubonic and black plague time that delayed mankind's progress for awhile.

Chapter 2

Our predicaments have continued regardless of our intellectual progress

Everyone wants something and then more and more. It's called greed and it's also called growth. To have more, one must do more to get it, right?

Early man crawled slowly to find food due to his amphibiously short legs. He learned, by moving faster, he could get more food. Evolution of growth sprang longer legs and arms which permitted more options to find food with more speed. More evolution of time grew intelligence to survive with more satisfying amenities of survival, social life and opportunities to progress in life which was very slow for many thousands of years or more.

During those years of slow progress, mankind wasn't promotion minded except for their natural instinct of bearing children. That was the beginning era of time when mankind was more human than of their pre Stone Age appearances. Man's desires grew with time.

Mankind's noticeable progress began as their fears of exposure to other human species slowly decreased through the system of bartering of which a more civilized approach to social exchanges slowly materialized. Instead of stealing from one another, many times through hostile encounters, they began to understand creative methods of sharing more peaceably and formatively as the ages unfolded in time. Unfortunately, they didn't become creative enough to plan for maintaining the future of mankind.

Once the formidable process of dealing with each other became easier to tolerate, the wheels of progress continued to roll. The cave man days of communicating were over and newly evolved homeosapiens became what is now known as mankind.

Brains were developing faster than ever and so was progress of historic recording. It was inevitably forming for what had appeared to be a more fulfilling appreciation of cooperation between the human species. Was it maturing in the right direction? Let's see.

Time rolled by again through periods of farming, boat-building for traveling and exchanging handmade products for barter exchange. All this enthusiasm created desires and ambitions to compete in an actual growing industry of exchange developing families of all nations. Sounds great; the good old days, right? It could have been if it wasn't for rising amounts of greedy people who wanted more for less and were willing to step out of bounds by ruthlessly cheating to get ahead in life. True, some felt they "had" to because competition was growing at a fast rate and the opportunities were wide open to pursue.

Competition was always a good source of promoting growth for stimulating civilized communities of people and their causes. However, the world of people didn't know they were on a slow, but consistent verge of creating what would eventually become a bonanza of unplanned riches, luxuries, world expansion, conglomerate business and leadership domination along with the opposites of staggering poorness, slavery, wars, multiple sadism and all the new and further forming technology, in the general sense, that has been and is consuming our planet of natural functioning and spitting it out to eventually end in a dead mass of rock and sea water that will be useless because of no living beings or plant growth to use it after we are all gone from the effects of occurring disasters mankind has brought on from hundreds to thousands of years in the past.

Yes, those are our predicaments of which are headed toward our described destiny at our present rate. Competition and growth are needed to handle our present needs and that is a large part of what can be our paradoxical downfall. What goes up immensely high always comes back down usually uncontrolled. That is also why this gloomy forecast is described as such. There was no master plan of any kind as the earlier or later ages of time have passed in what "is" appearing to be an inevitably crude and sad ending to what "could" be a healthy and stable world of living beings. This is only part of the gloomy scenario. Our progress is moving in a defeatist direction in a haphazard manner and we must correct it!

Sure, it can all be changed. The question now is are we ready to get serious in this matter of surviving which does mean sacrifices for this effort?

Presently, we are not. That's why this book must be read completely by many as a requisite for every individual to gain and spread consciousness of what "has" happened, what "is" happening now and what most signs of what "will" happen as time passes. "Then" we will know it's time for us "all" to act. This could unfold sooner especially since most of our population doesn't realize our present trend of survival is seriously threatened.

Our survival into a stable future requires us to move along much faster than we have been. Our general and predicamental progress is moving along faster than our cure for it.

There were obviously many very wise people who could visualize what would happen in the future from repeated habits of their socially influenced nature to want more for either staying up with or passing by others on the newly forming "rat race" humanity was creating. What those wise people either didn't know or failed to fully recognize was nothing would change the direction of man's destiny without concerted effort in a plan for human survival. Now we are faced with it. There is no avoiding what we have to do now!

One of our worst predicaments of the past, present and hopefully not the future is how mankind is spending or maybe wasting precious time, energy and resources galore promoting constantly improving necessities for living in the now only and not preparing well enough for the future of our survival on this planet.

Stepped-up scientific research has now revealed the predicament of climate change and global warming we humans have caused is going into centuries of time and is estimated "can" become a reality possibly decades or sooner than previously figured. If that happens, it will occur in most of our lifetimes and we are not becoming seriously or enough concerned about preparing ahead to offset that possibility.

According to the research, which was announced on a PBS documentary February 2012, it can begin doing its damage in just a very few years and not slowly as science has previously described weather changes over the millenniums.

We have a once in a lifetime or maybe even an eternal opportunity to speed-up the preparation for offsetting that total dilemma now, but will we do it? This is what these chapters are covering; to shake people into getting serious about our survival and mankind's future. Read and spread the word for our lives ASAP.

Spreading the word for our lives means get prepared to win against what "we" have done to create the problem, not spreading the word so people will give up as though there is no reason to live and resort to irrationally exuberant behavior which may hinder the progress intended. That's important to consider.

Chapter 3

The movement of progress before its plan

Who do we blame for our progress moving in a defeating direction? Well, we of early mankind did. That surely means we of the latest mankind must clean up the mess. We are, supposedly, a lot smarter now to do the job. It's like we went out for awhile and let the kids have a house party. When we returned, the house was left in shambles. We had to straighten it out. That's what mankind of the past has left for us. We either straighten it out or we perish. That's what this book and this life is about now.

Long ago, mankind learned how to go out and harness whatever they wanted like raising animals to eat or sell, grabbing land to keep, opening an illicit business, having too many spouses, naming their own rules and laws and endless other desires. Now they include spending hordes of money inventing new products for almost everything imaginable to make life more distracting, confusing and unreliably controlled and they haven't realized it.

The only plan they had was to make money to spend on more products or services that supported the wheels of needy progress which would likely be food, liquor, legal and illegal drugs, motor vehicles, homes, businesses, sports, hobbies, politics and a quandary of commercial and industrial material and parts for everything that moves and appears to serve human purposes; all mostly to support the system of which has become unbearably out of hand to the point where almost everyone is hurrying and scurrying to beat the other guys before they know what happened like a slowly gathering hurricane of people bent on destroying themselves. Added to that reality are the miseries of illnesses due to environmental contamination, contagious diseases and poor health consciousness and maintenance running amok around the world.

True, the deaths from all those factors does and would reduce the population expansion. However, if we allow that uncaring method to solve the overpopulation problem, that is not only immoral and disrespectively unintelligent, it is also defeating our more creative abilities of raising our standards for the purpose of preventing human annihilation. So, copping out from facing our responsibility of changing our world ways will only sink us in further to dooms destiny. Got it? As we pass through these chapters, we will more clearly see all mankind's past and present contributions are adding up to our destiny of doom unless we act now to avert it and continue being determined to change our ways.

Most of the past wars, which now goes into thousands of years, were results of greed for land

and power over the people, hierarchy and family disputes, protectionism and revenge; all of which were somewhat readily instigated mostly by ignorant, greedy, noncaring and immoral justification. The instigators only considered what "they" wanted, not what was best for the overall and perspective cause of any design of the future. No one really cared about anyone else's welfare and existence other than their own. The exception being where money, position, power, glory and neurotic love influenced them. This has constantly added to our present destiny.

The ancient and middle ages moving forward in the time direction of our recent industrial age was somewhat geared and instigated by magnetism of growth. Opportunities sprang up everywhere. Some were incentively created by forming communities, some were formed discovering precious metals, coal, more land for exploiting and many were formed for teaching basic, philosophical, political and religious subjects. Soon came the craze for transportation other than walking and horse back riding. Horse drawn carriages were devised along with dog sleds, boats and finally motor vehicles, trains and airplanes of which has, again, magnetized our present destiny.

Each one of the increments of progress added to the craze for having more of everything they could conjure up. It was all coupled by creative imagination, invention, acceptance of the resulting products and services plus overwhelmingly developed desire and in many cases, greed for more; like making money.

Most of mankind's historical and up-to-date progress may seem like it was all worth the effort. Judging it all is not the issue here. Our present chaotic struggle here on Earth as a result of it all is the issue and it "is" approaching. Read on.

Unnecessary progress of the world's past had inefficient planning or in many cases no planning and has become an issue much ignored in that past. What we do, regardless of whether we view it as helpful to our future causes or not, is how we become pretty much the same as what we eat is what we become.

The past is riddled with poor or no planning from so much of the time individuals who devise products, ideas and services that only purport to stimulate temporary solutions as getting a loan, finding a mate quickly, investing without proper knowledge, believing before understanding and proceeding with anything without gathering perspective of which is needed for preventing temporary and long haul satisfaction; particularly in this case, for preserving the present and future of invested efforts to survive.

Billions of people have run the wheels of progress for too long of a time. Sure, we need them for stimulating and growing purposes, but we also want those growths to "add" to the overall health of our societies, compatibilities and continuous existence into a stable and secure world of living beings, not a deteriorating future of humanity leading toward their end.

The "plan." as mentioned in this chapter's title, wasn't very well put together by caring organizers to say the least. The planning for a world of a secure future was only instigated by a flock of newly evolutionized and metamorphically transformed living beings now called humans; so it goes in the textbooks they or we have awkwardly created over the obvious eras of time. Think about it:

Visualizing if we had it to do over many thousands of years ago with only a few people on Earth having intelligence enough to handle that comparatively small population, we "could" have caringly planned with insight enough to have blended in with a simple concept growing, maturing and expanding in a natural functioning manner along with the obvious evolutionary changes in our planet's growths, stagnations and other unexplainable inevitabilities of which we now refer to as the ecology of living organisms related to and with our environment. Now, that's only a "view." We, of the aggressively planning nature, apparently lacked that little spot in our brains which could have changed the course of mankind's direction.

Was it "our" fault, the environments fault, God's fault or was it just the tendencies and forces of our universe's nature? Only each individual can speculate what and where the responsibility originated.

Now though, we have acquired a little more knowledge along with our obvious naivety so we "can" change our course of mankind's destiny of which is only a few hundred thousand years late, more our less.

These first few chapters are preliminaries on what had led us all into a mess of human deterioration of and for our future. Each chapter forward will lead to more of what is creeping up on us and what to do about it. Keep in mind, though, we have all been quite lazy in preparing for preventing a possible end to humanity. As we read in these chapters, we must gain more consciousness of that annoying fact. We wouldn't have had to face this oncoming deterioration of earth's protective ozone around the globe which is allowing the sun to heat up the earth's surface if we had accepted more responsibility and sensibility in controlling our constant lust to take away, add and rearrange everything on earth only to suit our desires of acquiring as much of everything we could have while we were and are alive and not consider what it may cost in misery for our people as time passed by.

That oncoming heat is a global condition and is increasing at a rate of speed where it will multiply as time passes; especially if we don't get with it now and stop or at least slow down the cause. This is what we are exposing in these chapters. Repeating in some cases is deemed necessary for retaining purposes with many or maybe all readers. Let us all stay ahead of our oncoming fate by paying more attention to its functioning and volunteer to help our cause of preventing our end. This book will reveal the bottom line cause of it all.

Chapter 4

How we used our intelligence for and against our causes

Everyone inherited their brains in some form from an earlier evolved time of man's origin and only inherited intelligence enough to survive against being eaten up by other forms of life larger than them. The passage of time allowed them to grow larger and smarter for that survival. They finally reached their full height and we are still being eaten up; not particularly by animal jaws, but by misguidance, deception, trickery and lack of in-depth knowledge of which to perceive and care enough about the type of growth moving forward into the future necessary for feeling secure about that future. That's humanity. Now we need to direct it.

Our educational system has been stimulatingly great around the world for so many willing people to expand their minds and look forward to more money, fame and position in life. It all seems the right thing to do, but they (we) don't seem to possess knowledge enough in using all that brain power to reduce the runaway conditions of world chaos including global warming, nuclear contamination, political and personal incompatibility, stress, strife, greed, selfishness, overcrowdedness, new kind of wars and the need to explore the universe for more of everything to extend ourselves beyond our present needs and aspirations. That displays indications of ruining us all and the pleasant, quiet and peaceful existence it was at one time when world threats and extinction wasn't so preponderant.

Most of us are reasonably comfortable with the basics and normal amenities of our living quarters, our families, friends, occupational affiliates, food, abilities to freely move around, pay bills and collect money too etc., etc.

Being too comfortable can also create anxiety to want more of it and more of everything else; if we can. Wanting more is an emotional magnetism to what is out there for availability and creates more desire for more. That and those ambitious states of mind usually do create work for stimulating economies of the world for growth purposes which, of course, is needed to prevent stagnation and recessions the way we have been so programmed in believing which has had such a profound influence on the way we act.

However, emotionally driven decisions usually have an effective tendency to only last for short-term satisfaction pertaining to the objective. A planned business, marriage or any other meaningfully desired relationship usually doesn't go far when it is instigated or inspired for gratification of the moment or short period of time which can be months as compared to years etc.

Mankind and/or individuals who have contributed to industry, politics, sales, families or any other cause to be productive are the ones to blame for the scary condition of mankind and other living being's survival today. Why? Brain power from education and experience has been increasing multifoldly since mankind's inception more now than ever with new technological advancements moving along almost faster than mankind can handle it. We "do" see that, right? One thing has led to another without a break in time.

Have we progressed intellectually enough to stay ahead of what may happen if we are replaced with robots and living manikins? Sure, that may never happen. It's something to think about when we see other things of nature going to pot such as our once beautiful oceans of the world being treated like junk yards, the animal life in the sea and land becoming extinct, how we are not able to escape the contaminated air we breathe and how the clean and fresh water supply is diminishing around the world; plus the unfortunate manner we are denaturing the land we grow crops on which will only get worse with our present population, ignorance and destiny.

Brains are straining all right for speeding and progressing with everything imaginable for one's immediate family which seems to be all they care about like speeding it up just to live for now. That's the direction brain power has been heading and getting worse.

Everything sped up usually gets there before anyone is ready to manage it. That's the brain power happening for the time now. Pessimistic? Cynical? Realistic may fit too. Our better future depends on how realistic we can view what "has" happened to what may or "will" happen as time passes.

Use past wars and sports as examples for brain power going amok:

There was more energy draining brain power used in all the human wars including all the materials, bloodshed and miseries than all the peacetime coexistent efforts of the species and for what; just to redirect human activity within newly established borders so they didn't have to spend brain time negotiating or dialoguing for the families of all the people similarly to how people unite in a democracy. We must redirect our worldly mannerisms.

Certain competitive sports have also had detrimental hindrances of brain power uses. Back in the days of the Roman Empire, brain power programmed the highest peak of excitement to be blood shedding to the ground and around while men died in agony. Animals were also brain programmed to compete for meat, one might say, just to entertain the audience in their battles to survive.

People in Olympic games have spent too much brain and physical power organizing and training to be top notch entertainers just to say they won while destroying their bodies for other pleasures of life in years beyond the glorious time of their participation only to build future legacies of corruption, greed and mistrust.

Football is just as bad in all their glory with all the brain power planning and programming. That's a twenty to thirty year career that leaves most of them broken down for what's left in life similar to many soldiers returned from battle.

Brain power can make or break a person, a nation, a business or a cause in general depending on how it is directed.

This author views the experiences of history as lessons which were directed by too much emotional objectivity mostly for monetary gain which led to more emotional objects of desire and not enough objectives for stabilizing the human status quo, their environment, their security, contentment and their better future.

Each of these chapters are adding and heading toward a more meaningful consciousness of which may be instrumental in changing the present course of our human and earthly destiny from a disorderly and disillusioning end of which we have all been responsible for one way or another without being consciously aware of it.

Each one of us has contributed to our locality or other areas of our world in our small or large manner and that affected someone and something else and so on from one to the next. This is partly why we are "all" involved and we can "all" change it with our brains. Don't let that slide by. Think about it.

Using brains for greed and super power may have been okay or even necessary for earlier times of mankind when they needed guidance. Now, in the past century or so, we are getting better world wide cooperation to correct some of the old time brain errors, but they are too slow resolving them without key factor help from the people of the world. This is what we are moving forward with in these chapters little by little.

Unfortunately, once again, the terms of moving forward have the possible misleading connotations of speeding up the process. That's part of the dilemma we all face which is to become more aggressively involved and now we "do" have to for correcting our ways for surviving.

Remember this when saying, "you can't win:" We are now much more advanced in our time for being able, capable, necessarily and even reasonably close to being desperate in checking and correcting our old time mannerisms, philosophies and approaches of which has led us to this confrontation of world stifling in one disaster after another including the two greatest threats of overpopulation and climate change; overpopulation being the inciting impetus of which has contributed to that phenomenon of climate change.

It isn't specifically or only where we can whip these major confrontations, it's a matter where we "have" to whip them or they "will" whip us; all of us and it's too close to just be thinking or talking about it. Our human generations got us into this mess and we have to get ourselves out of it or face the music of terror and termination.

Regardless of the fears or confidences we gather or the pros and cons we philosophically or religiously rationalize or conjure over, we must become more interested and involved in the most common cause we humans have ever experienced; our survival.

Chapter 5

Genetic inheritance, cultural influence and government control hasn't been enough to change world deterioration

The people still kept with basic necessities, but only with expansion in mind, not particularly with raising and maintaining secure, strong and lasting standards of living along with that expansion.

Old time families of the world were run by dictators and did what they were told by their leaders who controlled them with an iron fist. The people's incentive to work and be cooperative was based on fear of heavy penalties such as being placed in unbearable confinement, enduring torture and other abuses. The people continued living with old-time habits of which they were exploited by. Key factors to change our deteriorating world destiny of humans will be different than of the past and will work for future minded people. Let's nourish every possibility in that respect.

The democratic societies of the world can at least remain at peace freely with some limits in staying out of jail or be banned from societal affairs. Even with their freedom, they and their leaders too are strapped and confined of knowledge and fortitude to change our world of deterioration of which we all caused.

Now, in 2013 and forward, it seems half of the world's countries, if not more, desperately want changes for the future, but will probably settle for changes of the present which has been a historic tradition just to escape from the past conditions that lured them into the same old rut maintaining the status quo. We need to teach our young people to think more about mankind's survival which means to plan for their future security in everything they do for bolstering human survival, not world domination.

Nothing seems to inspire and excite the people as a whole community of the world except the possibility of gaining money or more money. More money because of greed usually kicks back.

With all the trials and errors of the past eras of time, mankind may not consciously realize they (all of them) need to move ahead and beyond their present mannerisms of cultural, societal, genetical and monetary influence so key factors can be put into place for the long run that will excite and enhance everyone to contribute toward a world of people who won't deceive, cheat, steal, undermine, cross or overwhelm each other. It's time to raise that consciousness.

This won't all be a grandiose state of utopia. That's a dream world. This will be a world of accepted reality and willingness to plan and sincerely execute plans of better value. The key factors we form along with the factors formed in this book have a great chance of this success materializing for our newly forming future.

Mankind is in a jam of uncertainty without a mutually agreed plan of "how" to proceed in securing a plan that will work in producing committed efforts which may seem to run against their "usual" ways. Usual ways for some are what is causing the problem.

Sure, it won't be a picnic for the lazy. It will be a huge world encounter of rerouting our human destiny. Our destiny of the past must be used for comparison purposes which will allow past progress to back off in exchange for new wisdom and intelligence for future endeavors. Indexes of the past will always be utilized for reforming specific areas of activity, philosophy and agreed on progress of them. We "do" know how to reform. We now have a much better reason for reforming which is staying alive.

We humans have been, are and will be forming a great many of life's lessons of the past and their foreboding disclosures for our use in constituting a plan for human, plant and animal survival into the distant future. Those are needed stepping stones for a path in avoiding human deterioration.

Our ancestors grew and stumbled through life for hundreds of thousands of years in their awkward mannerisms to make our world a livable place, but weren't always so complete in their efforts to civilize mankind for the distant future. We have the chance to do that now. Actually, it's one of the "last" chances we have.

Let us stay open, unselfish and be cooperative with one another in reinstating a new and better destiny for our world of living beings by gaining knowledge and spreading news of our inevitable human deterioration toward termination of our species and others too along with being instrumental in how to offset that dilemma with suggestions from this book and other similar sources on this subject. Cause, effect and solutions are unfolding in incremental proportion throughout these chapters. Patience for absorbing, appreciating and possible proceeding to help the world's people will be appreciated by all. Stay focused on the subject we "all" desire; the one of surviving.

Further, everything we have done as a human species up to and including "now" has led to our present and near future of climate change and its terminal baking of mankind. Only "we" can change it to a lesser degree for survival; if we get with it faster and more seriously than we have. It "is" critical! That warming and continued population expansion will evaporate all the fresh water and all humans and most animal life will extinguish and die in a short period of time.

Chapter 6

How the rule of law can become a detriment for change

The rule of law historically has governed the manner of lifestyle with most people of the world and hasn't changed much. It has also prevented many minds from making worldly changes for specifics of mankind's survival. Rule of law "is" needed for protecting, but it also contributes toward a super game of which we all get vacuumed into; the game of limiting our minds to focus on present day activity and exchanges and hardly ever on the "most" important function of inheritance as world surviving for future improvements, not future deterioration. Too many intricate laws can subdually and quietly keep societies focused more on intricacies of every day interrelated exchanging as compared to a much more important function of developing guidelines for preserving mankind while adjusting to new norms for the betterment of mankind and "continue" with their interrelating exchanges.

A graph of human progress for the survival of mankind can be devised of the past along with a new graph of mankind's progress for future survival based on our attitude, desire and plan for being helpful in gaining meaningful and broad perspective for purposes of inspiring the cause of human improvement where a better world of humans is desired. That is something to look forward to.

Law intensity or stated otherwise law enforcement hasn't decreased much because the uphill trend of the world's population has increased uphill since mankind became civilized and family oriented with very minor decrease in that population figure. The people then had no idea of how the increasing population would cause so many hazards ahead in their future.

The consequential results of human birth expansion has continually influenced and dictated expansion of everything connected with human progress and their relentless habits of thinking and pursuing; even their steadfast mannerisms of "If it ain't broke, don't fix it!" That's an old advertisement joke, but it sure applies to people hanging on to old-time habits because they apparently feel somewhat secure with them as compared to suggesting new laws that support the issue of keeping the human species alive.

The mind-set of experimenting with new issues hasn't enough strength and support for making a new way of life work well. We of the whole world must devise an equally agreed upon plan of changing our detrimental attitudes of cooperating as one world of people who will prevent all human deterioration, stagnation and eventual termination of all living beings along with procuring and producing a more mutually agreed manner of dependable stability for us all. That means all nations and people must come together closer than ever before to whip the problem we started long ago.

The laws of the past have served their purposes and they can be altered to serve and support the purposes of which the people of the world are all faced with. We must all decide because of our lust to survive. That's better than becoming victims of choking to death because of our increasing bad air, frying alive because of scorching temperatures or falling victim to drying up because of no fresh water of which mankind would use up quickly when climate change sizzles all of what is left. This is for real!

We can change it all and alter the rules of law for encouraging the people to enhance new lifestyles for the sake of perpetual stability and staying alive while supporting a healthy and smarter cause.

Let us create laws that will support a will to make better standards for surviving; even for those who have been engaged in illegal activity. Show them how helpful they can be instead of how resentful, desperate or just anticooperative they can be. After all, we are now all in this doom or survive situation together. Those who think they aren't can still be helpful by joining.

Let us adopt and/or devise laws, rules, guidance or whatever it takes that will encourage better cooperation between nations and any other groups or individuals who will enhance our worldly brotherhood and sisterhood with international aspects of respect; not limited, for instance, to special interests and sorority type groups etc.

World expansion, at the rate we are headed, will only intensify the rules of laws for more punishment, killing, mistrust, power orientation, selfishness, greed and less respect for others. Is that what we have come to after all the efforts of the past? We can and must change it all before it gets completely uncontrollable. Then, we will all be asking, "Why didn't we do something about it when we had the chance. The opportunity was right there in front of us." That's what this book is doing; reminding and guiding.

The overall people need laws, rules and guidance in a general manner; especially when they are expanding. They will literally "step" on each other to get what they want or to just get ahead of the other ones. Winning over others is about the same. One will feel good. The other will feel bad. Is that all necessary?

We (all of us) can change the greed and hostility by all of us agreeing to and focusing in on preserving and developing human survival because of its threat to humanity and our counterparts.

The jest of world contention, cooperation and agreements of how to arrive at strength and flexibility in laws for regulating promotion of survival activity is one of which has to be brought to the attention of all the people to vote on so as to prevent political gridlock. That simply means the "people" of the world must work with the legislatures in forming a more centralized method or creed of survival control for objectively procuring, maintaining and assuring the success of survival efforts.

Those efforts put forth for gaining the survival of mankind to need backing by strong belief, effective but not defeating civil laws and the support of all the people who will have formed the move for survival.

These moves for survival will eventually supercede old cultural tendencies of ignoring future security of mankind's survival and the new survival mind set consciousness will retain as a new way of life along with other "usual" amenities under reasonably agreed control.

Hang in there for the love of survival. This gets more interesting as we move forward in the chapters. Each chapter incrementally issues past, present and future key factors which are and will form a base for a guidelined plan that will be instrumental in offsetting mankind's present destiny of doom. Stay focused on it.

Be aware, when and wherever new laws are promulgated; especially as a result of lobbying or rallies, opposition can also form from nonsupporters who don't believe in the issue submitted. We must be diligent in preventing or offsetting that possibility for success of our cause.

Chapter 7

Religion's unaware contributions toward mankind's present dilemma

Democracy and freedom of speech is being embraced now more than ever in view of how so many societies and nations have repressed those natural functions of expression for centuries to millenniums of time in our civilized areas of the world.

The mind expansion factor of education is only as effective as the student of that education is allowed to absorb the knowledge taught. The more open and uninhibited the student is taught by the teacher via the institutional dogma, the broader the expansion of mind will occur for perceiving and learning what may be applicable toward the cause in any religious subject, belief or objective.

Religious education has its barriers for determining a manner in which to logically believe in and support. The religious teachers are defeating the purpose of being open for spirituality and expansion on "it." Religion has its limits. Spirituality has no limits.

A school class of psychology, science and religion together or all three separately offers a fair and nonpartisan view to compare in analyzing and deals with thoughts, feelings, perception and has many possibilities for analyzing. Science deals with accumulated facts and material substances. Religion deals with man written stories of a spiritually "led" universe.

Religion is based on, so far, a belief of a hypothetical image referred to generally in most religious sects as a supreme Being—or—God of which has never been proven or disproven to exist.

The historically established religions of the world will not broadly, psychologically, scientifically or even logically in much of any manner submit dialog of answers to anything of which may "expose" their historically gathered religious beliefs for fear of their organized regimes toppling similar to how the ancient Romans and Jewish hierarchy treated Jesus because of their fears of losing power over him and everyone else. They will also not submit dialogue on their much indoctrinated fear of not going to heaven if they resist or abandon the rules.

These mentioned fears have been strongly and almost dictatorially ingrained into the religious educational consciousness of billions of people over the millenniums and have emphasized religious domination around the world. One might say religious domination would very well guide the world's people to gang up on the nonconformers left. What would be left? There would be little room left for "real" open minded freedom to think, speak and exercise "any" new possibilities for choosing alternatives in any society other than rules of religion, that is, in what is presently referred to as the conventional manner (generally agreed).

Sound scary? People talk about creeping socialism which can lead to communism. Well, religion has been slowly creeping in for thousands of years, which actually is very little time since mankind began and has swept vulnerable, gullible, fearful, power hungry and other needy people into emotional and mental states of consciousness by the organized perpetrators who had their reasons to contribute to the cause or were common freeloaders riding on the cloud of hope to live forever somehow only through belief.

There is a difference between religion and spirituality. Religion is believing from organizationally established rules of believing. Spirituality is chosen beliefs within the self with no inhibited rules and can be interchanged with any other belief system.

Religious influences and pressures have had certain peace and comforts of mind, but also have been contributing slowly to enslaving mankind into becoming a superpower of which makes them prejudicial against freedom to think, believe and delve into and oppose any other manner of perception than the conventional manner of being set and believing their way only.

The power and belief in religion has been known to stand behind and support the military in battle as though the "lord" was the leader. That isn't factual; only a belief. The "lord" couldn't be the leader on "both" sides. That's partially where the overall conventionally guided people of Earth have been "unaware" of a perspectively clear picture of misguidance. Let's look for what is real.

That view isn't just in war. It's in everything where people must have their "own set way" without respect for others who may have equally good thoughts and beliefs as the conventionally religious type. What "can" happen? The one's who have acquired the slow and steady power through masses as the conventionally religious have, can, as time passes and at the present rate, suppress, exploit and gobble up the balance of society. There are strong appearances of this inevitability unless everyone freely and unconventionally understands the present and ongoing development of mind and is willing to change their ways of being pulled into this contagious black hole of deception. Everyone now admits the world of humans is going squirrelly. This version of spirituality, which is only one of them, is part of the reasons the social, biological, metaphysical, ecological and all the other cals have become deranged to the point where no one seems to know what to do about it all except to let the "lord" handle it. That can mean no one or anything has "any" overall control over "any" of it. How can we form a new destiny without accepting responsibility for it? We "all" need to accept responsibility and control over ourselves.

This book is about preventing any such fallible, deceptive, misdirected or even undirected destiny of human survival; definitely not to be interpreted as political takeover for power and profit as similar "promotions" have in the past. They may unfold again in time after and as our surviving existence becomes stable for new and more meaningful regulation has been agreeably accomplished. When that time approaches, mankind will have learned many lessons for survival and administer more appreciative methods of managing politics, power and super control over others.

Believing in something, someone or anything else is a necessary function of all human beings on Earth, but it must be individually utilized in a manner of freedom to choose when options and alternatives have been gathered for the benefit of freely choosing, not as a result of influences and pressures applied by parents, teachers, organizations and other exploiters for what "they" dominatingly believe in. Those attitudes are diminishing by the years.

The market of spirituality is littered with advertisements of creeds which spreads throughout societies of the world and prevents variations of truth, openness and more thoroughly understood reality. Now it is open for change. That includes the organizations too. Conventional religion has had their time in the limelight. Now, let the same people contribute something extra meaningful toward the salvation of "living" humans from oncoming chaos. More critical and survival data is following in chapters ahead.

Chapter 8

How and why mankind has been a poor predictor of the future and the growth of the past and present

We have seen the vast struggling of mankind on Earth through history of man's evolutionary, social, personal and spiritual growth. Everyone has the right to believe and practice with their existing state of mind of course. That's the best part of how we all interrelate regardless of being right about our claims and beliefs or not. Let us at least agree on that! The right to think and believe the way we "choose" must be maintained and nourished throughout the world for the existing direction of which mankind may stray into. Presently, we can all see multiple chaos coming inevitably because of our habitual past and present mannerisms.

Since all we have for predicting the future and basing a contention as "right" is what we can guess; all those supposedly expert predictors have done is just that; guess. Facts are much differently interpreted now than they were thousands of years ago.

The know-it-all and crusader type wise men, at least from the past to the present, have had strong tendencies to be pessimistic and spread the word about how terrible the state of human progress "can" or in some cases "will" be as time passes. We can see now where some of those predictions are unfolding in a general sense because it wasn't too difficult to estimate the future based on self-centered ideals and promotional attitudes of the past. Their predictions were and are not magical, supernatural or divine at all. Prophesiers were only guessing! It also isn't really too difficult to do when one can put together a few facts, incidents of human nature's tendencies plus a little simple mathematics that will indicate when these predictions will occur. They won't happen on the exact dates. People know predictions are only estimates and the believers are willing to wait only to forget about it when it doesn't occur exactly as predicted with the knowledge things change over a long period of time and so do human minds.

Many, if not all, past prophecied occurrences have become such strong beliefs, it's been like programming to happen and any similar occurring incident to what has been programmed from the ancient past seems to be interpreted as documented inevitability and people fell for it because of habit to believe. Now we have scientific research behind our claims. Truth can now be substantiated.

More up to date predictions can be just as misguiding, misleading and mistaken as how invaders from outer space will descend to Earth. Example: Organized looking lights were scattered over a U.S. city where the believers thought outer space people were invading. It turned out to be helicopters hovering still in the sky.

Other documented or not incidents of actors portraying messiahs from heaven ascended to Earth walking, talking, mixing with people which excited them for a time and eventually became faded memories in time. Nothing significant happened except for temporary excitement from justifying believers and heart breaking disappointments from others. Ordinary life continued about the same as ever.

Predictions of the past have suggested the dimensional disposition of our planets at a specific time will cause an end to our position in the solar system. The time came and nothing happened.

The patterns of human behavior continue fairly much the same as the millenniums unfold through the more recent centuries and decades etc. Sure, there are small and intermittent changes in new realizations and discoveries, but the general trend is still moving in the same direction which is to repeat the traditionally established habits of which have driven mankind to follow their trend of continuing to want whatever they can get as long as they can. They and their families, groups, governments and politicians or whoever else are alive really don't care very much about what happens to the future of humanity with their only now attitudes.

We have all been enveloped into an incongruous state of perpetual irresponsibility for "future" purposes. It hasn't been corrected and it "isn't," at present, being corrected in that sense. Deception, lack of discipline and caring about our future of mankind has to be at the forefront of mankind's drive to survive and we have been defeating that purpose left and right for a long time.

Prophecying and all the high tech development and fortitude behind it will continue based on the past evidence of mankind's progress to change for the better probably won't change much with past and presently repeated plans in improving mankind's survival. Moving toward possible changes for the better is what we are leading up to in these chapters. All hope for a more stable future is not lost yet. We have plenty of people on the globe who will support this cause. We just need "all" the people for a guarantee of human survival.

Prophecying must be eliminated and transformed into responsibly disciplined and realistically planned and arranged procedure for gathering worldwide impetus for human survival. The world's people must acquire awareness of what doesn't work from history to what is a better manner for survival into the distant future.

All people, governments and dictators of the past from those days forward have lost track and have failed to develop systems for future survival. They have all been primarily focused only on what each nation, group or individual has desired with not near enough strongly and adaptably coordinated effort in said world survival.

Mankind has made more mistakes in surviving for the future than any creative progress for that surviving future through being led by multiple guessing pertaining to many other areas of activity in the world as compared to considering the survival of the world's people and quite possibly all living beings and things.

We are all plugged in and associated with one another now in world exchanges and it's time to work together for the cause of us all. Consciousness of individual survival can be transformed into the survival of humanity worldwide. This is not just another way or method of anyone gaining control over anyone else. This is a "must" once again and as many times as necessary for the survival of mankind.

This book on what will happen to humans and animals on planet Earth in the near future isn't the same as ancient predictions. Ancient predictions have no basis except astrological indications or some habitual patterns noticed and interpreted by men who practiced occult like views of which they knew people would emotionally respond to as time passed. The predicted fate in this book is based on data from scientific facts and its supporting data which is now commonly known and not spooky or widely questionable for analyzing.

Men of the past have predicted the future and have proven to be a detriment to our future through unrealistic programming. Now it's time to plan and program what we will do for the betterment and survival of mankind, not loosely speculate which tends to mislead, deceive and become uncentrally focused or unfocusedly centered on any calculated destiny. Let us "make" our destiny! More focusing unfolds ahead.

Chapter 9

Raising standards is "one" key factor for our success in surviving, not stepping on others to get it

Everywhere we go around tall buildings, corporate meetings, banks and other places of business, classy restaurants, sports scenes style shows, museums, military presentations and a long list of well organized and polished appearing groups or individuals, we will notice a type of perfectionistic type of appearances. They are usually all successful in their performing endeavors one way or another. They are usually hailed, admired, supported and in ongoing demand to repeat their appearances. Why and how?

Successful people aren't automatically successful. They have spent endless time deciding, choosing, planning, arranging, adapting to and practicing their particular profession, trade or specific act. To do them well, particular attention must be adhered to in their efforts put forth for raising the quality of their endeavors.

Contrary to those who are successful are most poor class people who lack desire and energy put forward to strive, many times, in making decisions to develop themselves for some type of success or at least to be better off than they were or are. Those who were raised in a poor environment became "stuck" in it and most, but not all, were environmentally influenced to believe there is no way out. Some of them are lucky enough to scrape up mental energy in devising a method of which raises themselves into a middle class position of social and monetary wealth. An overwhelming balance of the poor sectors only produce a very few determined individuals who become successful in business, entertainment or politics etc. and make a name for themselves among being socially accepted, monetarily ingratiated and become ambitiously propelled. Those very few have raised their standards for contributing to world stability. It's just not enough, though, for influencing their neighbors.

What does this business of people's class or position mean pertaining to our literary subject of surviving into the future? Plenty. All this talk about high, medium and low class participation in our societies of life on planet Earth won't change much for the benefit of surviving into the future if we don't spend some time and effort in becoming a little more conscious about utilizing the "present" value of our state of affairs "through" these classes. That means "all" of them. They "are" the make-up and bread of social behavior of which is driving our safety of survival to the dogs, if you will. Higher standards among other factors for surviving are crucially needed. These will be viewed as we pass through the chapters. Taking notes as we go will add toward remembering and focusing.

The "class" of people's mentality, whatever it may be at the time, is what sets the standards of human consciousness of which, in turn, sets the direction of world stability or world chaos. We aren't animals. We "can" bring everyone's standards up without competing against each other. We must all help each other to keep the business of life afloat. If or when we get ahead by unfairly using others or "stepping" on them to get ahead, we will be defeating our purpose of staying afloat (surviving) and we will all eventually drown (so to speak) in misery. The odds favor us all staying focused herein.

Yes, this detailed lecture type is totally necessary with all its repeats. If we want a rationally and realistically stable planet of people for us who are living now and for future generations, we must exercise and expend more thought, consideration and energy toward raising standards with objectivity, insight, psychology, awareness, goals, caring, better health and living for reasons of mankind's surviving into the future. We must reduce thought and energy on the detriments of individual pleasures that only expands our contributions to activities of smothering our abilities to survive as a whole people of the world. They are creating more complexities that causes immense social, personal and whole world side effects which are excessively useless toward stability. More is elaborated on as we move ahead with these increments for staying alive.

Key factors for our world of humans are to gain knowledge of mistakes we as a whole people of the world have created and stumbled into by so many influences, direct orders and misguided advice, lies and unneeded education of which could have been exchanged or supplemented for knowledge of how to survive such as what we are attempting to do here and must continue to do as time passes.

Key factors are to raise standards of perception and insight for all of us to become "worldly" conscious in our efforts to blend with our "worldly" desires and goals for transforming an inevitably forming end of humanity to one of a reasonably stable existence with surviving constantly in mind. The forces to become extinct are great and we must offset them. Earth's atmosphere is changing and it's our fault. This whole book is working up to "why" and what to do about it.

Acquiring our success to survive requires all of us to do it! That means "none" of us will step on anyone else to achieve it or anything else. That's a win for all of us over ourselves.

Another key factor for our survival is to adopt a belief and be good examples of not cheating in any form in exchange for human survival. Everyone cheats a little and that grows too. Let's quit it.

The key factor of raising standards where people have been successful in their efforts, even poor to rich, can be valuable to use as a guideline for success in a career, relationships and for human survival. That's not difficult either; just keep practicing those acquired standards as a way of life and steer them in a direction they will help the most which, in this case, is mankind's survival. Acquire them in everyday accumulation and add to them in every way. When this is practiced as a way of life, that higher standard of living allows more significance toward an importance of being influential to others. Those better standards travel around the world and add toward more participation in world goals involving guidelines for all human survival by purposely, intentionally and cooperatively abiding by the very needed and mass chosen standards and guidelines established for the cause of our survival on Earth. It can work like the enthusiasm of a football game and "can" become a reality. That enthusiasm will grow as we realize how valuable our lives are.

Raising standards start with gaining knowledge and awareness of whether or not this is a valuable factor toward the cause. It begins and is chosen within the self, certainly not jammed into the psyche by any source of authority, group, organization or any other exploiter. This is all about freedom of choice and mankind's survival. When this transformation takes hold, new key factors such as presented in these scripts will arise with new and serious consciousness developing. Keep it going folks. It's worth the effort for saving mankind.

Improving our living standards for a reasonably compatible society of the world's people who are "willing" to pool our efforts for survival requires caring and believing our cause is worth it. That will work.

Chapter 10

The most outstanding detriments mankind ever made are still maintained grossly incorrect

Politics around the world is basically the same throughout with variations in their manners of controlling the people such as dictatorial ruling which has been known to be dominatingly controlled by one person and his power/fear laden supporters like Adolf Hitler, Saddam Hussein and Momar Kadofi. None of them contributed much of anything toward the survival of mankind; only the survival of them and their regimes. Dictating means telling others what to do in an authoritative manner, not really helping any needed cause.

Other than the dictorial politicians, the elected politicians, democratically or otherwise, have kept the people of the world dangling in apprehension concerning helpful world policy making and has also caused no end in avoiding the hindrances they have caused by not contributing more toward mankind's survival.

Democracy obviously means freedom to speak and choose by the people which, so far, appears to be the greatest method of community coherence. However, even that method hasn't proven to contribute much toward this more serious cause of survival.

Government's aims are to keep the people satisfied, protect them and prevent them from uprising against the government or their own selves, right? The idea of serving those favors for money is fine, but the actuality of "doing" those good deeds has intricate complications. Among them are: The politicians want the job and will do anything they can in their candidacy to get it. Why? They "do" believe in what they profess, but equally or maybe more, they want the monetary security and what the position will do for them in many ways as time passes. They will always get paid when no one else does. That's reassuring for them beside the glory experienced in the process. When all else fails, the politicians will be taken care of.

Next is about the joining of political parties and their seemingly inflexible and partisan mannerisms that deadlocks them together for rationalizing how to make laws and conduct strategic decisions for moving ahead in accumulated agreements. Hundreds of years ago, more or less, the decision for going to war was decided with the click of an eyelash. Now, war has to be "analyzed" to endless degrees that actually "causes" war. That energy "could" have been rerouted and focused on preventing it through other strategic and creative efforts nationally and/ or worldly with the study and practice of natural selection (survival of the fittest) and population control which would contribute toward less of a need to dominate and expand thereby creating less of a scramble for everything which is at the root of human problems from that point forward.

Beside making laws and deciding on strategic procedure, politics is the thorn in the side that agitates, aggravates and prevents meaningful progress of programs for creating world stability in human coexistence and survival. Politicians are suppose to do what the people want, but that becomes too complicated to arrive at with so many people, so each political party representatives interpret what the people want and focus on getting results from party philosophy which is a "belief" of how to make the machine of progress work. It takes forever to come together effectively. Meanwhile, the ongoing machine of progress continues uninterrupted because the politicians must abide by their political philosophy of keeping a job! Appearances are it's all about keeping a job for supporting and continuing the status quo of repeating expansion for making money and retaining group power whoever they may be. Survival of mankind won't be attained in that manner. We must educate ourselves to understand these cause and effects for proceeding with change to preserve our species of living beings and that begins on these pages.

Mankind's leaders have become obsessed with the selfish and grandiose illusion of being better off by grasping control of people and things, then expand everything possible in societies of people. This, of course, started a very long time ago and hasn't changed much. People have been emotionally, selfishly, socially and politically influenced in the momentum of mass desire to expand; many of whom recognized signs of power through expansion which would please their ever desires. Most others have been satisfied in remaining domestically engaged with employment and growing families of different natures and lifestyles. That's all about expansion of which is contributing toward world problems much of which may be very dismaying in having to face a reality where all this seemingly rewarding progress has unfolded over time just to erupt back into our faces as having been a severe detriment to our cause of, in this case, our survival as a people on planet Earth. Continue to remember, our planet is in process of becoming extremely hot! We have to get serious in offsetting that inevitability. Don't wait till it's too late.

There was a song back in the 1960's that said the world is on the verge of destruction. That version may be disturbingly true especially if we "all" contribute to ignoring plenty of signs being displayed these days where everything is out of control and moving almost too fast to regulate. The world is stormed over with people, pollutants, famine and killing the way it's unfolding.

The detrimental handling of mankind's survival is grossly off-key at present in its destiny. The direction of our survival must be seriously reevaluated by the majority of the world's people, but first the world's people must be more sufficiently notified of what, how and where our overall direction is heading and stay focused on an uncontaminated plan to change. This book is a contribution toward that knowledge and awareness. This author can only display the importance of the world's inevitable dilemma and hopefully inspire the masses to raise constant consciousness in forming a system of gathering changes for another direction. This consciousness must spread around the world to be effective in rerouting our destiny. This destiny belongs to the people and nothing or anyone else! It's up to us to make it work. Religious destiny is an uncontrolled and uninfluenced destiny led by belief only; not action.

The most outstanding detriments to our cause of survival hasn't changed much since money, barter and political power began which is basically to acquire and maintain power and influence "over" others by inflicting ideas and ideals designed to keep people in a position and state of mind where they won't even care to make decisions of change for fear of losing what they may have at that present time. Insecurity has been the driving factor limiting us from expanding our ability to make worldly changes for surviving. It's up to us to do it.

Expansion and growth, beside the disease aspect of the words, has traditionally been the encouraging manner of becoming at least promotionally better than one can be or for some, only better than they were. Let's use expansion and growth of "mind" for supporting survival. Our mind power can change our present course of existence.

Expansion and growth for animals and insects etc. has been an innate continuation since their beginning with, as its seems, no perspectively detrimental affect toward their overall survival as a natural function on Earth. Comparing them to the extra curricularly complicated mannerisms mankind has developed over the evolutionary period of time, animals and insects grew along with all environmental aspects of nature obviously without tapping the natural function of Earth's raw materials. Mankind, though, with all their intellectual abilities, couldn't leave the materials or their minds as they were. They had to change so much of the planet's natural functioning of plants, animals and basic substances of the earth where it is now malfunctioning with continuous animal extinction on land, contaminated air, bad atmosphere, soil, water and of course, man's exploitation, dislocation and sheer mutilization of the world's ground materials which transform natural substances into artificial paraphernalia and world contamination along with many disappointments.

It all supports mankind's cause of expanding all their badly formed and traditionally developed habits of wanting more of everything including the worst enemy they (we) will ever have; more of us as of the horrifying aspect of our inevitable oversmothering population of humans. This must be corrected for our survival.

Originally, there was more animals and all was naturally stable. Now there are more people and the world of "all" living beings are in jeopardy of becoming extinct. Who and what are to blame? Sure, it is us and our historical mannerisms to date. The only way that will change to retain life on Earth as time passes is to change our mannerisms and have a will to preserve mankind. That means all of us. Governments of nations cannot efficiently and effectively direct us into a position of momentum for changing our mannerisms. They can only make new laws, proclamations and inforce them with penalties. We all must adopt new reasoning for new goals and stick to them. This is where we begin, along with many who have already started in the individual process of rearranging our conscious views of human survival. Selfish, noncaring and ignorant people "could" become our enemies. They will perish too.

Mankind is already correcting many technical errors around the world in all areas where they can be improved upon in industrial output, education, relationships, health, communication and generally the basics of life moving forward. They deserve endless credit for those skillful accomplishments. That's one side of the viewpointed coin.

The other side of the coin, however, questions why are we on Earth all headed in a direction toward oblivious termination or at least a miserable and torturous existence wondering why we didn't do it differently if we were and/or are so smart?

Yes, it's because our smartness has only had desire to constantly move forward with earthly gatherings and haven't nourished enough common sense in appreciating the living feeling of life itself which, of course, is our measly bodies themselves.

Which "are" the most important assets in our lives; things or our bodies? Pluck our bodies out of the scene of life and what is left? With that, let's start getting serious about what's important. Once again, the balance of other living beings will follow in our footsteps.

Chapter 11

Gaining views and insight toward transforming chaos to stability and harmony

We are learning about the problems and mistakes we are "all" really to blame for with these stagnancies and general chaos approaching us by "not" accepting enough individual responsibility of conducting our "individual" contributions toward "world" power in numbers and effort. Yes, each one of us individually constitutes a much greater power when the amount of those people are added together than "any" dictatorship, democratic government or organized religion can direct, by far.

We can utilize that "free mind" power within each one of us to change the existing inevitabilities for serving the cause of survival for "all" of us including animals and smaller life.

Dictatorships, unified empires of past ages and recent party led regimes have exploited the minds of nations for conforming to the cause of those leaders, but no one organization has ever exploited the minds of the world's people as a whole for "any" worthy cause as surviving with much less expanding population.

Now, all of us have to assume the stance and objective of arriving at and promoting a workable system of which "will" turn our present dilemma into a world community of ongoing survivors. No, this is not about political philosophy or party driven crusades. It's about people influencing a new way to survive with less of everything.

Even the dictators, free mind governments and religious powers won't battle each other on the issue of everyone surviving as compared to the entire wipeout of humanity. How? Be patient and read on.

First, as number one, we must "all" come to an official and unequivocal agreement where the life survival of humanity takes precidence over "all" other activity and decisions on this planet. We are all doomed if we don't do this first. Even though this may sound like a ridiculous expectation with such an immense population, we can do anything if all our lives depend on it. We deserve this opportunity to save our species. When we all think in this manner individually, something great will happen. It will be the greatest and most dignified world-wide community effort ever tackled and that will prove mankind "can" work together and accomplish great strides for survival.

If there is a large and organized group of people on the Earth who are determined to annihilate mankind and even themselves by systematically promoting their plans in that effort, our solutions for the survival of mankind may experience a detrimental hindrance and a foul cog in the moving wheels of preserving and promoting mankind's plans to survive and work together. It may be a little rough to begin with. We may have to influence or alter the seemingly strong and unconventional belief where killing and suicide is a solution to the world's problems. Conventional belief and wisdom professes mankind is to live and deal with problems rationally for creating a compatible world of people similar to the way animals and insects have done for at least millions of years. They didn't screw up the ecology. Mankind came along and did it in less than a few thousand years; more in the past few hundred years and even worse in recent years. Coincidently, the population explosion has comparatively occurred around the same time as human and worldly problems have become more threatening. It seems there is a connection.

Conventional wisdom, in general, seems to have been drifting away from the scene of rationality, intelligence, peace, quite and caring for our fellow man as it so previously appeared back when philosophy, science, goodness of religion and societal integrity seemed so prevalently important and meaningful. It has all transformed into a vacuum of incoherent and abusive consciousness that momentumly influenced mankind's presently appearing destiny of doom.

We "can" exercise a purposely developed method and plan to offset the negative aspect and results of our human tendencies to eliminate ourselves through constant reminders of changing our ways as these chapters on this important subject iterates, professes and reiterates throughout. It is accomplished by repetitious determination.

Coming together for developing these purposes of surviving will be accomplished through the auspices of mass agreement that will roll along like a ball of snow and gather in many different ways since it is made up of many different people. The formation will spread and magnetize people into it like cool air into a hot desert because it means survival. The desire for human survival will grow and inevitably lead us into it with patience just as anything else worthwhile does. It will become a pure and innocently motivated movement to alter and modify an ancient system of civilization that ran astray and amok for which "could" have been thought of as a flourishing horn of plenty, peace loving and compatible world of living beings, but it didn't. It got out of hand! Now we can bring it back into reasonably good focus and function through all of our collective efforts. For now, let that be an introduction of what we must think about doing "before" we leap to high in its initial process. It's not an election for public office. It's a process of becoming informed, choosing, believing and becoming a part of future survival in any or whatever way we can in being instrumental in that effort. As we all grow in this process of consciousness, we attract more of the "right" branches of participators who will help spur the process of human survival. Again, this is not primarily for the purpose of expanding any organizational, institutional, political or capitalistic ambitions or promotions unless they are agreeably adjoined in the movement of pursuing human survival.

Number two in any official agreement of survival is another concept and needed movement in world cooperation of which is stated in the next few paragraphs and appears to be the biggest threat now.

Speaking of cool air in the desert heat, we as world promoters and cooperators must apply more serious determination in supporting the climate change issue by individually, as well as jointly, cooperating with community and world coalitions in their efforts to slow the stifling progress of greenhouse affect which isn't getting enough attention to prevent broiling us all alive in a few years. This is only number two in our efforts to make totally necessary changes, but it may just be the largest threat to our survival. Read your author's book entitled "Offsetting Climate Change And Nuclear Contamination." It's full of contributing thoughts for helping to significantly reduce the warming effects over time while governments and industries work on programs to stop the trap of human termination we have put ourselves into. Yes, we have done it, not God or nature.

Remember, global warming or climate change, as it has been referred to more recently, isn't affecting us greatly now, but it surely will when it accelerates to a point of no return or no possibility to stop it. This can happen in a period of our lifetime as we accelerate our progress and expansion. Those years are derived from recent scientifically researched estimates from the early years of 2000. It's nothing to toy around with.

The never ending drive of progressive expansion or expanding our progress, as it may be, is an excessively and overburdoning task where mankind bit off more than they could chew. Now it's beginning to cause a sooner than later doom where everyone may drown in their own vomit of lust, greed and desperation from waiting too long to correct their previously propelled destiny.

What happened with mankind you ask? More gathered awareness in number two continues as follows:

This is about the greater majority of people on planet Earth with the exception of the millions or maybe more of the very poor, the down and out victims of genocide, slavery, undefended, unknowingly exploited and so many others who were circumstantially unfortunate in developing their lives. We must help them join this cause of survival.

Most people of the world, without knowledge of it, have been programmed to believe and act the way others in the past have. They felt they "should" be as good or better at the usual activities of life, so they learned the games of life, took chances and gained what others had. Then others gained more and they also had to gain more of whatever their programmed desires sought. It never quit.

The progress of societies grew as it was obviously planned by the programmed people of the societies through suggestion, need, greed, envy, making mistakes, making money, competition, egoism, societal pressure and expectations all expanding "too" fast with technology, programs of science, war and the promotions of education to learn how to stay with the normal trend of world progress "and" in particular, how to accel in staying ahead and maintaining a dominant position over others. Oh yes, let's not forget the most important issue of it all; the irresistible urge and developed drive of "lust" to do more of it because of the ongoing momentum of its progress and because not enough people are reducing that progress.

What has it all led to? Right; an almost inescapable "rat race" that ends in stifling disarray of life which is even difficult to imagine. Will we allow ourselves or our offsprings to witness this inconceivable tragedy? That's what human progress has to offer if we continue on this track of historical to present day progress. See your author's books entitled "Paradox Of Progress Unfolding 1" and "Paradox Of Progress Unfolding 2." They are insightful stories relative to this book's contentions.

The progress of expanding up to date has only been thought of as putting people to work and maintaining the existing status quo. This is still focusing on gathered awareness for preparing a world agreement on steering world chaos away, but before we continue, let's view a significant factor of detrimental causes:

The relationship of climate change is cohesively tied to the gargantuously developed industry of oil that can be a key factor contribution toward the progress of mankind's annihilation since oil runs so many industries in the world and the demand for it is still strong. Survival depends on their cooperation too.

World societies, products and service industries were growing at a somewhat unaware consciousness for centuries until they discovered what oil could do; in particular when they became more acutely aware of what could tentatively be an unending supply of it. After that, inventors and scientists leaped into a frenzy indulgence of creating machinery galore for a brand new way of human living. It became a new age of spoiling the consumers of things and gadgets they never even dreamed they might "need." Of course, they also never dreamed this new influx of products for the household, transportation and endless other paraphernalia would trigger "another" booming industry now known as technology which would set the world aglow in a glutinous rat race for more of everything even if it meant stepping on others, so to speak, to get it all. The oil industry became what appeared like a golden industry where mankind could have almost everything they ever wanted with and through that greasy stuff. Little did they realize though, at that time, the seemingly huge opportunities they were casting among themselves were to eventually become a monster of horror when that golden liquid would lead everyone to an impending disaster just waiting to happen through its contaminating affects on Earth's air, water and temperature that would wipe mankind off the surface of the planet through the scorching heat and squeezing masses of panicking human beings. Next is another hazard:

Their are so many influences and factors entering into the confusing issue of what is the most detrimental contribution toward world stagnancy and failure to function in a stable manner. Here is one very close to the top of them all that began many hundreds to thousands of years ago when one couldn't wait to buy or barter in exchange for a product or service. It has been referred to variably as a debt or loan of credit or trust. Now, it is more acceptably referred to as, you know, a credit card. It was an innocent manner of exchange in its beginning and continued very supportingly for many years until a magnetism of desire for more of everything slowly began to infect an opportunistic ridden influx of newly forming businesses, gold rushes, migrators, emigrators, imports, babies of all nationalities and everything else born, made and workable that progressively engulfed those newly forming masses of people to expand without any central focusing or helpful guidance. That passion spread around most of the world like a slow moving tsunami or "any" contagious disease. Tsunamis and contagious diseases do their worst and fizzle out shortly after, but not the unprepared or even unorthodox movements of so called civilized human beings. They kept surging ahead with their progress of expanding in almost everything they have done. Unfortunately, so much of it has been adverse functioning to our cause of maintaining human life with less population.

Earlier in the history of world societies, various sectors of human behavior begged, borrowed, swindled or stole whatever they could. Up-dating those days, most of these typical or average eager beaver type people finally discovered a surer, more profitable and much safer method of procuring monetary exchanges other than being scoffed at, scorned, arrested, fined or possibly killed in the process. Yes, it was the credit card. It served as a convenient manner of quick purchase and supported the expansion of rising debts which have reached an unprecedented proportion of multiple indebtness by tapping more into the credit allowance for purchases at a much higher rate of interest creating an infectious habit of living financially beyond one's capabilities to cope with. This all adds to mankind's end.

Contract borrowing is usually managed under strict control and hasn't proven to be financially threatening with equity possessing people when its arranged with income to payment proportion. Over extending on contract borrowing is unduly risky and negatively adds to detrimental world expansion when the masses are doing the same with the vulnerable money system thereby attributing to the expansion of runaway debts, civil instability and civil disobedience.

Credit card, contract borrowing, pawning and the like in lieu of paying cash has been contributing toward desperate intentions and risky expansion of all the business, government and personal indebtness mentioned in this book. If this continues, life will be hard.

So far and up to date in 2013, the people and governments of the world believe growth and expansion is the prime solution to a healthy economy and when in a healthy economy, everyone will be reasonably satisfied. That has been the traditional contentions of success for a long time and seemingly has called for more of the same to date. That may be true for those who are content with the belief where now, the short term measured in months or a few years, is all that matters and any other period of time has no meaningful value because of life not being very long. We "can" make it longer!

This is one of the most significant factors of why mankind is going down the tube unless it is checked and corrected now! Societies of mankind cannot survive much longer only living for what they can get for their immediate time in life. That means the future of living beings is also following that historical pattern and has, is and will become only a temporary existence on planet Earth unless we change; now!

However, if educational progress and human expansion has taught us anything about caring, sincerity and meaningful value of humans, animals etc. and our earth under us with all its value, there has to be plenty of thought and reasons for all of us to rearrange our individual feelings, views, insight and desires to support ways and means of improving human maintenance of our immediate, ongoing and future survival. This is accomplished by gathered awareness of our past to our present and gathered insight for conquering our past inabilities and developing new abilities for change, prevent power dominance and greed in this effort by showering cooperation for our cause of survival and "not" supporting noncooperating people who care less. More groups must be formed for open, sincere and supporting dialogue for survival.

Progress and expansion began and unfolded as a contagious disease a long time ago without conscious observation by the world's masses of people. The people have responded to whatever the master-minders offered and didn't resist the temptation to become the bloodsuckers of opportunity, industry, progress, expansion, religion and all covert exploitation of which they now refer to as normal tendencies. It "is" truly that; normal, addictive disease. We are now beginning to see and experience the "king daddy" of all contagious diseases; the blinded venture where mankind started the psychobiological and psychoneurological disease of which has destinated our future from its beginning. It's called passive/ aggressive victimization; for the lack of a better description.

The necessary course changing elaborated on in this book will take effect if and when the people become scared enough to face their own reality of becoming victims of runaway circumstances mankind fell into long ago which became a nourished ignorance and caring less of how our future would unfold. Facing it and caringly dealing with arrived at solutions partially offered in this book will free the bloodsucker's connection of mankind's susceptible tendencies to slip, slide or fall into place by slicker and powerful influence.

It's up to each one of as to regulating our tendencies while sharing our influences for the cause of survival. We are now at the point in our history where we can take our pick to create our survival or experience the end of humanity and our animal counterparts.

Now we are also at the point in these chapters to gain more awareness and remember not just to read the chapters, but to grasp on to what is important, significant and meaningful in this cause of human survival. The last chapter is the leading source of gathering the facts, points "and" humble opinions for deciding whether or not to join first the individual cause to change for human survival. That's where it starts. Later, it will become a new and reasonable manner of coexisting with others who want the security of life sustainment.

Now is the approaching time to put it all together in chapter twelve for open and broad analysis of the power each person can gather for spreading the word of what "is" the right destiny for mankind; to fade away because no one cares or continue building nature's smartest species on this planet who really do deserve a better chance for life; a chance we all have to make. Governments can only help. It's we who have to do it first within, then together as a whole. That works. Put it all together conscientiously and it will work even better. That state of mind always did and always will.

We of the world are way overdue for coming together in straightening out our undernourished and self-centered abilities to accomplish a strategic act for the basic survival of mankind and other living beings on this planet. Let's drop a few of our wasteful needs and adopt our need to survive!

Chapter 12

The solution and results will fall into place upon their properly fitting contributions

Among the preceding views mentioned toward very difficult times ahead, the present rate of world expansion is one of the "most" difficult challenges we have to deal with. It is with the very sensitive, emotional, traditional, inherent and innate subject of propagating the human species which appears to be running excessively rampant as "the" largest detrimental factor and contribution toward mankind's abilities to survive at the present rate of birth volume. There are eight billion people on Earth now and the forecasts are to double that in just a few years. That is not "just fine" in any way shape or form. Maybe it is for people who live only for now with no caring desire to improve our state of survival and have mankind live into the future with a contented and stable environment in "any" era of time. Now is the time to turn a future of massive chaos around, not down the road when it gets real intense.

There was a time on planet Earth when overpopulation wasn't thought of and certainly not an issue to be necessarily considered. People were developing languages, learning how to travel, forming methods of bringing more food into hungry forming societies of the world and always preparing for war along with their everyday chores of maintaining what they have acquired. Little did they know what was ahead.

Appearances are they were also becoming more passionately driven while wanting more of everything in their areas of emotional encounters including sexual intimacy and the desire to have babies which, of course, meant families and it happened. What else happened?

Now we look back and we can see too much was beginning to happen without anyone noticing. The wheels of progress were rolling into a storm of human expansion that would eventually put mankind's survival to a very life threatening test. It was about what the passion of desire, sex and expansion would bring as time rolled by.

New children entering into the societies of the world needed and/or were showered with essentials and as much more of what parents, teachers and opportunities could shed upon them thereby teaching them the ways human's "should" follow for the next many hundreds and thousands of years more or less. This has followed suit generally as either the natural tendency unfolding "or" as it has been said, was meant to be. Obviously, there was no one or thing planning or leading that uncontrolled escapade of ongoing human expanding momentum and is still perpetuating; only much more than ever out of control and how many bother to be seriously interested in it?

The desire and need for more of everything has created a reactionary influx of problems as well as pleasures. Expansion in endless endeavors of progress and existences of good and bad families, politics, social life, business, love and romance, law and freedom and a host of other national and international complications have caused sped up dissension, tension, mistrust suspicion, overcompetitive ambition to take over and dominate people, business, nations and spiritual belief. Unavoidable involvements have expanded without much relief in thousands of years while much more has in recent hundreds of years with more uncontrolled acceleration now than ever. Why? We are now entering into facing more reality in the raw. Get ready.

Let's keep reminding ourselves it all started with the acceleration of the human species; mainly the uncontrolled passion for intercourse and traditional desires to build a family for emotional, social and coherent stability which could be referred to as neurotic or false security (real security is either taught/learned/earned or developed within). Want more security? Reach out for more reality.

More intercourse inspires and creates more human power within and desire to expand it in as many ways possible. It does so because it is a natural process of utilizing energy as similarly discovered by S. Freud in his studies of psychoanalysis where all human energy is sexual energy and we humans have certainly used it to an overextended degree! With eight billion people, that may only be a start of overdoing unless we make some drastic changes.

More people entering this world of relentless growth in every way are causing more needs for more people which is causing more "stuff" for more people to create more of everything and then more people (children) are conceived by more self-centered people as has and will expand causing more of everything which will, in turn, consecutively and relentlessly cause stress, strain, disease, eventual starvation from inept management and wildly erratic land and weather differentiation, environmental contamination, loss of fresh water and less room for all these people who are living longer now and will be adding to the ever growing population only for them to inevitably suffocate with every last living being on Earth in the most miserable manner one wouldn't want to even imagine. So far in these scripts, that's only "part" of what is forming around the globe. Now, in the centuries of two thousand plus, the oil industries and their supporting government, all their combined employees, associates, distributors and consumers can't seem to wait in producing, selling and buying the high priced stuff for burning up the roads, the water, the air and all the oil running machines and technology of our world's industry all for the benefit of snuffing us out because we failed to plan better and sooner.

Do you think all that is bad? The worst part of it all is how much faster it will occur when the momentum "really" increases? We must become deadly serious in making changes much sooner than as soon as possible. When we reach the time limit for no return, there will be no stopping the end of our existence.

Then before the end, when there are maybe a few million living beings still alive, they will be suffering with the stench of possibly hundreds of billions of bodies everywhere until those people become the same. Too bad we won't be ready to exit the Earth on a venture toward another habitable planet like in my mentioned book of "Paradox Of Progress Unfolding #1" and #2. We are too early for that and our present destiny won't allow us to wait that long. We have gone too far with our progress of selfishness, greed, ignorance, pleasures and fantasies and not enough of gaining more consciousness for passing on and training our young people to think, plan, believe and crusade for the survival of the human species while automatically preserving all other living beings on the globe.

Now, what do we do to accomplish the task and necessity of this reparative adventure on planet Earth?

We need to refer back to at least three of your author's guidelines for bottom line changes. This is of course, only one manner of approach to stabilizing our world's conditions. Super greatness would certainly follow if many creatively skilled people would submit similar forms of change in groups for this challenge of reforming an old and lost cause to a bright new and stable future. The following is "a" method for that desire:

1. We must all form, believe and agree meaningful change for our survival is necessary and has to be implemented very soon. This starts with everyone realizing mankind will only survive on this planet

if we all join together as well as we possible can while we understand the seriousness of our present destiny.

Our world of people have "never" formed "a" world community for reasons of human survival. Most communities, groups or nations have formed mainly for strengthening their "own" cause of improvement in their "own" neighborhood, state or nation; many of them with the idea of consuming their world neighbors, dominating them and exploiting them for their "own" benefit whether it has been accomplished by dynastical rule, religious power, political idealism or outright war to take over. All of this has contributed toward our present mannerisms of greed, resentment, misguidance, misunderstanding, enemy, deception, self-centered and sadistic consciousness of which has led us into this illusively perpetrated ordeal. We must make strategic changes to avert the worse.

Each one of us must acquire a mind-set consciousness of world survival, not the same mind-set consciousness for individual survival only. That will only alienate any possibility of humanity surviving. Individual survival is not the same as individual consciousness for survival. See last of chapter eight for that difference.

The time has finally reached us when and where we must all think and believe ourselves into alternating our worldly political systems of leadership that have only supported the dominant functions of power over the people and not enough into supporting the necessity of power for healthy survival. This pertains to the masses of people, not the few elected representatives or self-chosen leaders of domination.

Sure, most of them are very well educated, but most of them are only educated to help promote what they believe will keep the people calm enough for supporting the causes that "keeps" them calm and regulated so those representatives can continue maintaining their regular positions where all seems well for them. It isn't working too well anymore. What would we do without making changes?

The people and the leaders around the globe have been and are suffering discontent with one another and want some kind of major change regardless of what it may take to achieve it. The problem is, no one knows how to make changes that will please the people. Maintaining the lives of the people will certainly please them. Let's get with it! It's gotten out of hand like they say and we have to do our part in conjunction with our leaders "primarily" for survival. This cause of human survival may be the common denominator that brings the people and the politicians together for really solving problems. We just need to step it up a little faster.

Which is more important for the people, to make changes for more money and/or what may seem like better conditions for the now mentality "or" be more concerned about the continued existence of a more contented human species of beings? Survival begins now with those two questions. So what is it we really need to do? We, the individuals of the world at present, need to raise consciousness of what is needed and wanted and if it is primarily focused on the survival of mankind or whether there is either not enough focusing or no focusing on it at all. Focusing and staying focused is powerful.

2. Also, on making changes for survival, when we gather enough consciousness for majority or more agreements to where human survival is "primary" on the list of determined objectives, striving more on one of those objectives will definitely require worldwide cooperation. That objective will never be needed more than now in curtailing the most annihilating contribution to mankind's extinction. What is it? Get ready for the classic mind

blowing contribution ever inflicted by humans on humans without them even knowing it. It is the never ending, most sought after and irresistible pastime urge to pleasurably and exuberantly procreate for increasing the population of the world which has spread rampantly throughout more infectiously than any other ground species in our known history. Sound crazy? It "is" crazy what has happened right under our noses and now, because of the selfish contributing factors of so many humans, our surviving existence is threatened to end in massive misery. More of everything has been our contributions toward the progress of human overpopulation. Everything which expands without control will surely break down somehow by stretching, sagging, becoming adversely ill and expire. We can already see what is unfolding with overbulging body weight. Continuing this epidemic of expanding body gobs will indirectly add to the detrimental cause of human extinction in massive blubber drowning where those who will still be alive will be too sick and weak to care about processing the dead. This is all contigent on whether it happens prior to the dehydration period of global warming or not. Being dehydrated "because" of no fresh water and extreme heat will certainly shake off the fat if there is anyone left. One way or another, we will all be gone soon after if we don't act, once again, now or very soon.

Control over birth conception is a total must. This is a huge part of changing our survival consciousness, ideals, passions of intercourse and family production. If we don't, this world calamity will accelerate to unbelievable and unbearable proportions. We must become more serious or there won't be anything to become serious about anymore. Isn't that enough to get serious about?

Getting individually in touch with what we want on preserving our human existence for the near and distant future requires our attention in crusading for birth control around the world. The people of China are now the pioneers and leaders of this effort in their country. They know reducing the population can prevent the chaos they were threatened with at one time.

Intercourse for accidental "or" chosen purposes where there are no limitations are stifling our efforts of progress for maintaining a peaceable, compatible and harmonious world of humans, animals, fish, birds and the like. Being selfish for the life of lust and uncontrolled family satisfaction is now empirically and logically inhibiting our chances of survival which is causing too many unfulfilling demands and expectations of all natures. Soon, at the present rate of expansion, the domino effect and progressive chaos will unfold with, again, uncontrolled attempts and will be too late to handle. Pessimistic? Negative? Maybe. Do we want to make another big mistake by believing that way and not crusading or is it better to put forth effort in reducing our terrifying possibility of extinction by reducing that which has caused that bad habit potential?

This book submits and promotes raising standards for reducing overpopulation while reducing the continued uphill "trend" of reaching a precipice encounter where and when we will all begin to fall, so to speak and there will be no turning back. Okay, see this situation as being similar to a graph of the stock market trend of ups and downs. The stock market so much represents human life. The market of business stocks started over a hundred years ago as business investments for making money and grew into a healthy business for entrepreneurs and investors. The established numbers representing the up and down progress did move up and down like life's encounters. Sometimes it moved way up and people thought it would continue, so many held on to their stocks. Being just like life, the people became very disappointed at times because the value of the stocks dropped precipitously and the share holders lost gobs of money. The greedy and so-called "savvy" investors lost until they learned how to play the game of life. Many of them learned, settled for less and made money, but not as much as they expected. Most of them didn't learn the game of life which is, in this case, what goes way up seems great while it's moving, but most always crashes down and leaves so many people dangling, disappointed and suffering because they didn't crucially, rationally and conservatively prepare for what could be financial chaos and also for what could be more losses through their greedy methods to capitalize.

The stock market, however, has managed to survive quite well "because" of its volatility. Each crash became a time of relief and adjustment that prevented a possible end to that type of investing. The crashes were only a few notches down on the general trend upward which allowed a healthy stock market forward.

The progress of humanity from the beginning of our urges to grow and expand has and "is" similar to that of the stock market and of course, any business too.

Mankind's history has been overladen with steady, unresting, relentlessly plagued uphill and expanding progress to the umpteenth power. It seems like we "have" been and still "are" acquiring everything we think we need. Alas, our expanding progress has unfolded too much like the stock market only without a break or needed rest. The basic and major repetition of progress occurring on our world and in the vast depths of the universe "have" and "are" dependably and consistently unfolding in a similar manner. What could be a more reliable substantiation of how "we" are repeating enormous feats of progress. Unfortunately, mankind's expansion of progress has gone too far "up" to maintain ongoing stability for survival and hasn't consciously encountered enough purposely regulated "down" adjustments which creates healthy progress for healthy survival.

Part of our success in surviving into the future depends largely and primarily on each one of us being separately stable within and staying focused on changes as this book recommends plus being instrumental in influencing others to do the same. If one is not stable, now is the time to correct that mentality wherever possible.

3. Making changes for survival: We must all gain more perspective on the issues and problems that has led humanity to the brink of what appears to

be an eventual end of mankind by listing all or as many factors concerning problems, confusion, frustrations, greed, desires, misunderstanding, misdirection, passions, enviousness, hostility, selfishness, recklessness, impatience, intolerances, aggressiveness, stubbornness, uncontrollability and out of hand human pursuances to acquire, receive from, control and dominate over others thinking that is what is needed to accomplish anything in this life; all of which has and is contributing toward the end of us all in each one's incremental way.

Fully realizing those incremental contributions in an overall perspective where the fault of this chaotic condition on Earth is directly connected to everyone having lived on this planet in some small way will allow the balance of us who are alive in accepting the responsibility to move our destiny for survival forward.

Reversing the present situation isn't a fitting concept for proceeding. That will only send us back to the old detrimental habits we need to escape. Bottom line changing our ways (all of us that is) is more realistic and must be adhered to in "any" procedure.

Emphasis on all of us in worldwide cooperation is a total must. If and or when we "do" arrive at that consciousness through studies as these and others, we must firmly latch on and practice continuous, enthusiastic and perpetual maintenance of that effort extended momentum to steadily arrive at and in time for refurbishing a system of a much slower growing population, industry and general progress. During and beyond that great period of backing off and making adjustments for reducing our chaotic end, we must also pursue and maintain a number one insightful desire and requirement of preserving human survival for "all" on planet Earth, not only for the strong, rich and more capable, but for everyone. That's what we need for changing our much too expanded population. We need a smaller and more extensively "caring" population. It is being proven an excessively expanded population becomes a less caring population of financial deterioration, moral degradation and humanly caused environmental and ecological calapse.

The following is a list of summarizing notes necessary for creating a stable and lasting future for humans of which has been compiled from a long life of your author's observing, experiencing and studying the actions and reactions of human progress and vulnerabilities pro and con. Each one of these guidelines are designed for working up to a powerful method of change for those who want to be realistic innovators for this very needed cause of surviving. Let's get realistic:

1. Gather as much information on being beneficially helpful in understanding how mankind started,

motivated and prolongly moved the power of progress that served them while unknowingly leading themselves into a squeezing trap of doom in time. This knowledge must be comprehensively acquired for gaining enough reason to serve the cause of changing our present direction of an inevitable end; to offsetting that end in developing a world system that will eventually save mankind from that terrible fate of doom.

2. Brain power, as much as it has been developed for self or national centered purposes and expansion, has to be rerouted for awhile in supporting a more important purpose now more than ever of crusading for the cause of human survival. The educational system around the world can drop less important subjects and begin new subjects of meaningfully needed necessity for this cause.

3. The element, factor and psychology of caring has to be rearranged from tendencies to cheat, manipulate, mislead, swindle etc. for purposes

of selfishly gaining earthly control of almost "anything" to caring primarily for associating, dealing and engaging with objective and creative feelings, thoughts and ideas for promoting a stable world of humans for future survival. Industrial, commercial and other business promoters must also focus mainly on survival or they and their business will surely vanish from the face of the earth; all of them in a time all of us must realize will be sooner than later. The word "change" is usually phrased as a political or business maneuver for improving the system for its success. The most successful venture we can make changes on at the present time and forward is for human survival since "we" cannot make "any" changes when we are all gone at about the same time! Preparing "before" the chaos approaches will save us depending on how serious we all become, again, "before" we are terminally bitten by a merciless and overwhelming death we brought on ourselves. Humans have had incredibly strong tendencies to procrastinate on issues of grave importance. Now we must refrain from that manner of approach when tinkering around with mankind's survival.

4. Individual awareness of mankind's impending doom has to be acquired and remain at the top of the list for supporting the cause of rearranging priorities in this movement of world consciousness and change for survival. New individual incentive and habits for world cooperation in these efforts for survival are and will be critically necessary more as the element of time passes in a life saving race to see who or what will win. It will be either the intelligent discipline and determination of mankind or reactionary forces of nature.

5. Indeed, the efforts of this cause for survival will unfold in a positive and accelerated manner of our being the winners for human survival

much more favorably when we all participate in understanding the facing dilemma and crusade individually, in pairs, with group dynamics or major rallies for raising survival consciousness and their necessary changes for mankind's survival; all of which must be implemented legally by petitions and lobbying for legislation to regulate and help guide the people's wishes and demands for strict control of new mannerisms for survival. That's a must among other methods since there will probably be people who won't voluntarily participate, but still want the beneficial results.

The possibility exists where too much time will lapse in the procedures for survival and the people of the world may panic. We "must" stay ahead of that real possibility with more sweeping energy applied in these surviving efforts. Each one of these notes are gathering more success potentiality for a powerful initiative procedure.

This plan "will" work; especially if we "make" it work.

6. Yes, the individuals are the one's who will have to lead in efforts to combat this threat of extinction because of their power in numbers, not the governments of the world. The governments will take "way" too much time to do it. We'll all be suffering or dead before they can red tape a solution to embark on. Not only that, it is their job to do what the people want. Anyway, why would they not want to survive?

By the way, there is no need to worry about any voting process pertaining to our survival activity. Odds are no one will contest votes for keeping us all alive.

Let's let the people initiate this movement and have our governments perform their acts of participation quickly and without deadlock encounters. After all, the lawmakers and their families want life and business as usual to continue too. Without these promotions, they may not stay alive either depending on their time in office.

Crusading for a cause hasn't been traditionally very popular or even favorable for most people due to controversial differences, perceptions, attitudes and beliefs etc. However, we have never "all" been exposed to oncoming termination, so no one will have to suffer rejection of any kind for crusading for a most common cause of preserving mankind for the future; especially when they can be led to understand the future of "all" of us is dangling at the stake of finality. Crusading for "all" our lives seems a pretty good reason to do it. Imagine, effort put forth now in time will help preserve a much more stable and acceptable world population for millenniums in the future until they, once again, lose track of what can reoccur with human unawareness of previous expansion. Groups for crusading will ease the anxiety of doing it alone.

7. Preserving humanity requires doing it in many ways because the progress expansion of mankind and their many ways is what has contributed to much of what can be desired or craved like basically, money, credit, greed, material, drugs, incorrigible power, denomination, excess intercourse and motor vehicles and a list that becomes longer as mankind allow's themselves undisciplined tendencies and other ways of life with less concern about what we are now studying; the crucial necessity of coming together worldwide in devising common reasoning for a plan to reduce our expansion way down.

What so many people are also "not" concerned enough about is the win or lose factor of preserving their quality of mind and body. They do everything else in life while generally assuming good health is an automatic attribute from being born, growing up and supposedly maturing into a society of regular health beings.

People who purposely pursue and gain better health for the express purpose of living a long life have a very helpful attitude for contributing toward this cause of survival and hopefully their examples will inspire others to do the same. Good health, strength of mind and body can be contagious when survival is good reason to do it. That can grow powerful enough to help the momentum of defeating the threatening doom of humanity. Keep going. We are headed toward the ultimate reasoning and rationale for offsetting our threatening destiny.

8. All these numbered points of survival guidelines are leading up to finalizing a scheme of a most significant and effective platform which everyone can understand and agree "is" necessary for proceeding to spread the word of worldwide efforts in inseminating survival consciousness

by adapting to and practicing new and needed mannerisms "for" that survival. Hang on and hang in there for the world's most importantly meaningful project and adjoining necessity for all. This number eight guideline is emphasized as having to be way at the top of the list of priority consciousness. That means we must all, in our own choosing ways, spread this consciousness belief and determination so everyone else will be influenced to follow up in this very needed cause to survive. This will work. It just requires all of us to do it as is necessary to keep remembering. Mass momentum will get results. No one will resist because we will all agree except the few who just don't care for life.

9. Consuming drugs, legal or illegal, is very close to the most detrimental factor in combating our destiny of doom. More people coming into this life live under the misconceived belief they need drugs, so they get them and consume

more as time passes. Consequently, they place a burden on their strength of mind and body of which really needs emotional and mental strength for maintaining discipline and guidelines necessary in conserving and strengthening what is needed for a stable population of survivors. The exception is the consumption of articulately controlled drugs administered by professionals who caringly treat and/or prevent disease or illness.

Drugs, alcohol and any other addictive substance must be eliminated or at least better controlled for reducing physical and mental diseases. Addictions of any distructive nature must be seriously curtailed. Continuous use of all these disease makers will lead to poor health and as a result poor decision making contributions that may be seen as a hindrance to our crusading for survival now and most certainly later as time passes.

These guidelines are small to accomplish in comparison to what incredibly huge efforts on health could be as time passes if we pay only a little attention in exercising them. Hang on. We are building our platform for survival.

10 Humanity now doesn't like to admit it very much, but one of the biggest errors they or we have made throughout our decision making past and even more so now was and still is a most unfavorable passtime of making "mistakes." They have led us all through times of confusion and societal treachery where we couldn't determine the difference between so called honest mistakes and unscrupulous deception.

Now, with the exploding population, there are more mistakes made than ever where it is more important than ever to reduce them and is worsening any cause to stabilize human existence for survival.

All efforts mentioned in these guidelines will be adding to making less honest mistakes because our newly developed trend of progress will become less aggressively motivated therefore calmer decision making will allow less mistakes which will add toward a stable society of humans; the results of which will be noticed in the ecological environment as time passes. Mistakes cause more mistakes as we are noticing around the world and we can reduce them by "caring" to make these needed changes in making major adjustments for survival. Get ready. More significant guidelines are approaching.

11. Noncooperating and greedy people cause an imbalance in efforts toward stabilizing humanity as in the "war," if you will, on climate change. Oil is the biggest threat in that respect. They are pumping more of it with consumers demanding and using more of those products than ever. The producers, consumers and the rest of us

must become more life or death conscious, unfortunately, for cooperating in this need of better decisions for survival. That means cut back "greatly" on industry and auto uses etc. or die a very hot death! More oil, more people who need it, more expansion of them and everything they need more of are mistakes added creating more problems because of them along with whatever other surprises we may encounter means we haven't a chance to survive unless we "all" cooperate in these guidelines for human survival.

12. Moving ahead from the inevitable chaos consciousness mankind has created in the past to a powerful and oncoming consciousness for whipping the present and seemingly uncontrolled dilemma of human extinction, we must all improvise on a revolutionary system of shrinking our present system of expanding progress. It has worked awkwardly for too long of a time and is obviously headed into a "mistaken" direction.

It's up to us to stop the mistakes, correct them and lead ourselves into a less mistake direction as these guidelines suggest. These guidelines are not formed for political purposes. They are just looking at and facing mother and father reality for keeping mankind alive the best way we can. The central theme of thought must be for us all to stay focused on helping each other now for a change. This new system of survival "will" work for the purpose of surviving "and" raising our standards. Why would anyone complain about that? Joining together will enhance our success of survival.

13. There are too many people now who "bend" the laws of which have been designed to protect us. Those laws are needed more than ever with this expanding population. Those who "bend" the laws for their own purposes will be the next law breakers who add to the inevitable extinction of mankind. Those who allow themselves to go crooked are added factors to our days of doom.

They are anticooperators to the cause of human survival. The benders and breakers must be notified how they are indirectly adding to the forming chaos mankind started and are, at present, motivating and promoting its destiny possibly without them even realizing it. Everything is becoming so closely intertwined and connected from the ancient past to a present direction of mankind's obliteration where they cannot seem to see and understand the seriousness of this reality. Law benders and outright criminals had better be educated to understand when humans merge against average peace and social cooperation, it adds to a conglomerating usurpation of nebulously scattered and out of controlled masses of doom stricken people going nowhere but to their final destination; all depending, of course, where they believe that may be. Everything accumulated adds to that scenario. When they are led to understand the pending threat and realize flexing and flowing with their forensic attitude "for" human retainment along with all these other defeats of the past and fair possibilities of survival for the future, we will "all" succeed together for a better world of humans and our animal counterparts along with preserving the nature of our Earth.

14. Before we bring this lecture of numbered guidelines to a complete and what may seem a rather shocking conclusion, success in this world venture is totally necessary for all who are capable to participate by talking to others about this plan for survival while spreading the word as widely as possible so others will do the same and that momentum will continue as time passes. It must be a way of life and steady until we are all sure and gratified we have arrived at our destination for us and our ongoing generations of the future while they follow the new trend.

15. We are now approaching the ultimate necessity of our venture to retain humanity on planet Earth so our environment and ecology will also be retained.

We have now gathered enough information and consciousness awareness for understanding the negative aspect of problems with our expansion and also the positive of what we can do to correct the flaws.

The stock market example is typical, viewing their ongoing graphs, of what is healthy for a long life of investing in stocks as compared to gambling in stocks. The market is well over one hundred years old and is an "invented" business of which has had many gains and losses over the span of its life and is still moving forward. It will undoubtedly continue this momentum as long as there are people, money, bartering and an abundant supply of desire for more of whatever; which is not necessarily within the scope of our present goals on survival. Less of whatever now means more of survival.

Stock market history has shown quite regularly, through its time, where progress moving up steadily always makes adjustments of its value and the prices drop down. Generally, it does it from either bad news or from smart investors who sell their stocks "before the fear motivating value drops the prices down. Then, common investors follow the selling process by selling a little later forcing the prices down until they settle. The first seller made returns, the second wave of sellers broke even (more or less) and the remainders who didn't sell either took a beating or kept their stocks for the long-term with average long-term returns (usually less percentage return). That's life! All three of these investors can retain a healthy portfolio throughout the years by utilizing insightful, rational, knowledgeable and experiential wisdom. However, they don't all do it. The successful investors are usually a smaller amount of investors

and the remaining masses struggle with their dreams
of becoming rich, just make a living in the market
or fail constantly. That's life too. The market is still
a healthy business of money exchanges because of
regular and periodical adjustments downward. From
its beginning, the stock market has maintained a
steady seesaw trend up. The periodical crashes were
frightening, disappointing and caused serious distress
to many investors who had to start all over again,
but each time it crashed, the upward expansion trend
angle remained reasonably stable as it appears during
this writing of 2013. The only guarantee we have
in that continuation is how we insightfully nourish
its momentum. The same nourishment applies to
how we maintain our human lives for surviving in
an unprepared civilization. That's the reason for all
these references to the stock market. Once again,
the stock market is a good example to observe
in understanding how to prevent disappointing
encounters because of not preparing "before" they

happen. Emphasis must be placed on the value of these comparisons for supporting strength in our survival.

Not preparing is our most stifling and threatening issue toward human extinction. It's real. It's here facing us and we must pursue and win over that threat or we will all be goners sooner than later.

What else do we do beside what we are preparing for in this book and elsewhere? Firstly, we must clearly understand how relatively close the picture of the stock market trends of ups, downs and crashes are as compared to the ups and downs of our human expansion over a lengthily period of time which has been and is moving upward with very few fearful and opportune oriented adjustments. No one has ever thought of worldwide human adjustments geared toward the survival of mankind and yet mankind's expansion progress has and "is" moving way too steeply up for healthy comfort and life sustainment. Our human expansion is overdone and we are late in seeing it now. We must act A.S.A.P. to avert that chaotic destiny.

Secondly in what else we can do to prepare is, as realistically and unhandy as we may not want to view it, we must all apply short and long-term population reduction! Sure, that will take time to materialize which is all the more reason to start motivating and moving it along right away.

We, the earth's majority certainly won't agree to eliminating people like Hitler did because we would probably eliminate all of us and that would be like defeating the purpose of making beneficial changes for retaining humanity, so that isn't a viable solution even though many have not only thought of it, but have actually attempted it in nations living under dictatorial control. So once again, we must not nourish that as an option.

What is next in controlling human body reduction? That's right, the bottom line solution for reducing the human body expansion after all is said and argued over is to reduce the "production" of them as a method of healthy adjustments which are absolutely needed along with reducing our runaway and general trend of human progress. That may be somewhat difficult because of our strong desire and greed for that progress and expansion. We must use discipline in controlling that temptation of desire for human survival in our private lives and through internationally agreed birth control. Let's get serious.

Everyone must gain consciousness of what may be the most difficult activity for adult humans to tackle which is daily, weekly or whatever periods of time for sexual intercourse with or without contraceptives. Maintaining a "most" needed control over birth conception is an essential contribution toward reducing the population for shrinking the accelerated expansion of mankind's progress back to a reasonable point of adjustment similar to that of the stock market. This will save mankind from their terrible fate.

Now then, how can we realistically do all this extraordinary changing and shrinking back to a level of having "less" of everything when we have been so spoiled through the desires of endless growth and expansion? We can do it by reinforcing our goals of life retainment. Each one of us must adjust to an acceptance of reality where we would all die while continuing a complete fantasy of remaining alive through an out of controlled destiny mankind originally created. Now we see that hasn't worked for extending life into the distant future. We are close to understanding more how to proceed in this life saving venture for a sustained human existence.

Along with that continued consciousness of the mistakes we have made in the past of not making periodical adjustments, we can adapt and "remain" focused primarily on staying alive with slower growth that never gets out of hand. That becomes our assurance for future life retainment.

It "will" work, but it "will" be work in controlling our tendencies of desiring "too much" before, if ever, we learn how to environmentally handle it.

Climate Change, nuclear waste contamination, overpopulation expansion, oil contamination in more ways than one and other contamination too long to list is a battle we must "all" undertake. We "can" all do it with what we all have in common now; life.

The super game of power for the greedy and domineering may put a damper on our success and defeat the chances for humanity to survive into the future. Everyone must be aware of that possibility. Those kinds of people wouldn't stop at anything to support their power and dollar of which obviously won't have any value if and when we all perish.

One last reminder of what we are "all" up against: Our present destiny of doom is about our consistent contamination of our earth's atmosphere, our approaching losses of fresh water from climate change, our smothering from overpopulation and slow poisoning of what we consume which includes the quality of our food, other liquids, air and drugs etc. Now the farmers are having problems growing crops do to overpopulation. Starvation, panic and death will follow if we don't change. The intensity of them all, without reducing their causes, will be the cause of massive annihilation.

Let us not settle for mediocre results in this effort to successfully survive. That will only be trailing along "behind" the chasing monster of doom. We must be relentlessly diligent and determined in our efforts to attain and preserve humanity. That is accomplished by proclaiming mankind's survival is worth saving, worth believing in, worth crusading for and overcoming our evils, inhibitions, errors and vulnerability of being greedy, self-centered and oblivious to the desires and needs of others.

The essence and importance of improving mankind's nature for the purpose of surviving is a much larger and perspective view than just saving our protoplasmic existence for the present time.

So far, with our knowledge of Earth in comparison to other planets, we are especially unique with humanity, animals, birds, fish, plus squirrels, plants, fresh water etc. and the oceans around us.

Humans possess potential capabilities of which must not be underestimated for possibilities of communicatively engaging our skills with the solar system. Presently to the future, planet Earth and our solar system may be dependent on efforts and capabilities of mankind over and above any theologically hypothetic influence or supposed control of which no one has ever known anything about and possibly never will. Belief alone is not enough to build security of surviving. It requires gut level determination and "real" effort.

Our purpose now as humans for surviving is to help in every way we can to prevent a total end of humanity, reduce our expanding deteriorative systems of industries, economies, ignorances and most of all our uncontrolled volume of people down to a point of renovation for a new, sturdier and more stable society of humans who will reasonably assure themselves of maintaining slower, steady and more meaningfully controlled progress. Without that control, we will probably resume our previous mistakes which will ignite the expanding progress of the past.

Applying a new educational system of discipline and accepting more social, civic and personal responsibility for maintaining a stably growing world society for surviving is probably the best we can do for now and forward. Let's work on it.

When our population has decreased to a feasibly agreed point in adjustment, all other decreased progress will be settling with a much calmer society to and for maintaining a "steady as she goes" world of less aggressive and stable humans who will hold their course a little wiser. The results of our world's combined efforts in changing our ways, lobbying for trimming industrial pollutants and oil running vehicles plus controlling overblown birth expansion and climate change will be noticed for at least a comfortable environment and life will continue. We "must" stay diligent in those efforts and make it a way of life for our desired survival.

Nothing of any meaningful value ever moved forward without good reason for its beginning. This book is an added chapter in human ventures where the world's people now have an opportunity to form a better society of human species for survival purposes.

Remember the reason, impetus and criteria for this movement of change. It is not only for survival of the human species; it is also for making our cause, as a human species, a more stable and compatible coexistence with one another. The points and factors mentioned fit in together and must be adhered to as cooperation for that cause, not primarily the cause of your author who is only an instrument of assistance in our cause of survival. We are "all" instruments for that cause.

If anyone has any preconceived notions where climate change is only a cyclical phenomenon and passes through every twelve thousand years or so regardless of what mankind does, remember, the greenhouse effect and climate change was only noticed within a couple of hundred years or so and nature changes weather "very" slowly over thousands of years where no one would notice if they lived through it. With that, don't feel relieved where climate change is no threat to our survival. That will be a "gross" error. Climate change has happened much too quickly. It "is" our fault! "We" have caused it through our continuous expansion in everything.

If climate change doesn't consume us completely in the short term, there is a better chance than not we will all live in a worse imagined globe of torturous heat in hell as compared to a tied up bag of wild cats in an oven for who knows how long. Do we deserve that?

The following is "not" a prophesy of the distant future like those of the ancient times, it is a forecast of a relatively "near" future based on up to date scientific research and analysis: Mankind will expire if and when they can no longer breath do to lack of breathable air, fresh water, food and room to exist "because" of not eliminating the use of pollutant driven vehicles (cars, trucks, planes and ships etc), of "not" greatly reducing industrial contamination and of "not" greatly reducing the expansion of our population. They all work together against us in creating climate change phenomena.

The extinction of mankind can be deterred, rearranged and/or offset by adapting the suggestions and guidance from this book and others of a similar nature.

All adverse contributions mentioned in these scripts have added and are adding to this author's forecast of mankind's "near" future dilemma. These contributions cannot be made exceptions to our cause of survival. They have and are apparent dreams and aspirations where growth type expansion is the accepted standard of living and its progress. We must change this.

"The" last reminder: The most important key factor in this battle to save mankind among several others is to significantly reduce the present expanding population of human beings and maintain those positions. It "won't" work without doing that. Expansion of human beings will defeat our purposes of surviving whereas maintaining much less population "will" increase our success in surviving. Apparently, at the present time, individual and government control limiting the number of children born very strictly is the only sure method we have. That is where the people and the government must work very closely together to arrive at the best and earliest results. This "is" the most important attribute of all contributions toward our survival. Study that factor and realize how the demand for everything has increased with expansion of people and has caused the expansion of the greenhouse effect. Climate change is the bottom line result of too much expansion of everything and primarily too many people indirectly causing it.

I, your author, have learned over the many years I've been alive, to appreciate this life of mine and I've also learned my purpose in life. It took a long time to realize that. My purpose, after realizing life is only a one time venture, is to make the best out of my existence by helping the world's people to do the same and staying alive to do it. Writing on subjects as this book and many others allows me to exercise that privilege of maybe influencing others to take a little time for gaining a similar appreciation of living on this planet and maybe influencing others too for making the best of their lives by spreading this kind of word around the world through each one of our communities as suggested in the previous pages.

We are all different in our world and we all possess a potential to defeat one another's purpose and end our rare privileges of living or we can learn to understand more about each other, bend toward one another in a compassionate manner as people of Earth, not enemies and join in making the best of "our world's" people.

When we all practice this type of creed individually to overcome human extinction, we will come together like the flowers in the springtime and the water to the rivers. With incentive and effort put forth, our hostility to one another will lessen and we will finally be able to see new horizons of brotherly and sisterly adjoinment and earthly realities which will automatically, if not mystically, transform our threatening doom to a safer and simpler way of life. We just need to speed it up a little, once again, before it's too late.

Cutting way down on child birth is "the" most important requirement toward preventing massive and final doom of mankind. Everyone must cooperate. A "few" just won't be enough, unfortunately.

We can now see the natural disasters beginning to happen on planet Earth along with the terrible unrest and conflicts humans are encountering around the world. They are all brought on by overpopulation and the affects they create. It's up to us to change it.

They've been talking a lot about how ancient civilizations suddenly disappearing from their homes in isolated areas of specific nations with very little trace of where they went or why. At least we know, from the buildings they lived in and the relics and a few deceased remains, there was an organized system of human beings of who existed in an acceptable environment for years of time.

Now, with oncoming possibilities of mankind's doom, future apace travelers won't have much difficulty in determining what happened to the people and other living beings on this planet when they notice all the bones and dried up skin spread around the saturated amounts of vehicles and industries galore where they were left standing with all their energies dwindled to the last of their breaths.

Those travelers would see how the whole world of life killed themselves by waiting too long to stop it. They could have stopped it. They just didn't.

Even if space travelers don't come by for a feast of deadness, the bugs won't even inherit the earth they died in. The sun will reign in its glory.

Oh well, noncaring humans probably wouldn't deserve a fitting planet to live on anyway the way things work out sometimes.

Your author, Lloyd E. McIlveen, unveils a chronological list of many and various book subjects presenting controversial, educational, uplifting, futuristic, self-helping, philosophical, psychological, entertaining and other stimulating concepts of which are and will be displayed with brief descriptions of each book followed by more issues in line as they become published.

1. "Evaluating Outdated Beliefs" This is a report, viewed through the perception of your author of the evolutionary process and changes occurring in belief; especially in the area of religion and spirituality. This was designed for the benefit of broadening individual perception, perspective and viewing "another" plane of belief while revealing fallacies in theological indoctrination. This is an improved revision of the book's origin.

2. "Staying Alive On Planet Earth I" This is a psychology of health required to stabilize and maintain better health for the benefit of living a much longer life. Source: A lifetime of study, problems, recoveries and many successes more in natural methods.

3. "Understanding Loss To Relieve The Anguish" Loss of anything involves many distractions and disrupting emotional disarray. Gaining greater understanding of these emotions offsets the misery of them and enhances optimism of confidence and support for emotional weakness before, at and during the time of loss.

4. "Understanding Preventing And Eliminating Cancer" presents new views on the wonders of natural methods for practical use.

5. "Paradox Of Progress Unfolding I" This is a tale told by a man "many" centuries into the future about an exciting, overwhelming and terrifying occurrence on planet Earth as a result of their wondrous progress around the time of 2300 A.D. Hang onto your seats! #2 is a second issue later on the list.

6. "Offsetting Climate Change And Nuclear Waste Contamination" This view of the two exposes the hazards, inevitabilities and possible solutions

needed now for preventing a "too late" disaster that will affect all living beings too soon.

7. "What God Is And Is Not" This is a study of spiritual possibilities designed, not particularly to remold conventional mannerisms of belief, but to open and expand perception in the most controversial subject of mankind; the subject of God and whether mankind will or won't expand that consciousness along with all progress and growth on Earth and in the universe.

8. "Kids Of The Crick" This is a story of four old fashioned country kids setting out on a weekend adventure in their countryside of tall grass, mountains, rivers, animals, caves and strange living beings. Sometimes, they aren't sure whether it's all real or not.

9. "Paradox Of Destiny Explained" eliminates the mysteries, facades, fantasies and deceptions of how, where, way and when we do what we

do and opens new possibilities for expanding our beliefs and consciousness pertaining to this study of available options that may influence insight for growth, change or even justify present mannerisms of what may control the individual, planet Earth or the whole universe and is not zealous, fanatic or bigoted; only assertively revealing.

10. "Paradox Of Progress Unfolding 2" This book is a continued fiction story and can be considered exemplary of "major" human changes that alienated millions of people to another planet in the future. They are led by the elements of unexpected surprises of which is par for the course with gutsy space pioneers. The first "Paradox Of Progress Unfolding I" must be read first to understand and appreciate the disproportional attitudes and positions of people on a threshold of major change and disasters upon them. This is not only a tale of travel,

trials and tribulations, it is philosophically stimulating and adds toward future insightful expansion of the human species.

11. "Staying Alive On Planet Earth 2" This is all extended version of the original psychology of health for living a longer life. More knowledge allows more life.

12. "Preventing The Doom Of Mankind" This is a stimulating, vitalizing and somewhat shocking description of how mankind is "truly" faced with extinction in the "near" future due to their own faults of progress. It's very educational and needed now to help offset that inevitability where the odds dictate we will all perish if we don't adhere to this offsetting of which "is" possible to achieve.

13. "Spiritual Transformation Of The Fourth Millennium" Old-time conventional religion is fading. New-time spirituality is on the rise.

Objective realism is the prime issue here for future inclined thinking and believing.

14. "Understanding The Science Of Creative Mind" This is a study for discovering, developing and practicing a psychological powerhouse within for conquering the unconquerable, achieving the impossible or doing things no one has done all depending on, of course, the makeup and determination of the individual. This study brings out a greater potential of the individual's abilities when taken seriously. This was compiled from a lifetime of study and experience from your author.

15. "Living to 150" is a guidance program for intentions of anyone desiring a longer than longer life which is insightfully and innovatively educational for that purpose.

16. "The Act Of Getting One's Act Together" If anyone, business or nation wants to develop their stance, priorities and position in life, this

is a chance for them to get their act together more than ever.

17. "Making Changes From This Point Forward" The design of this book is for the purpose of preventing repeated mistakes of unforeseen surprises due to what we weren't or aren't aware of that did, can or will happen again. It's all about gaining or rearranging change consciousness in this area.

18. "Relationships For All" This is a carefully arranged view of how relationships can function much better when initiated or guided by the experiences of many experts and your author who have had failures and successes in their very human encounters. The experiences of more relationships result in wiser judgments and approaches to others.

19. "The We Between Us" helps us in discovering who is good for us and who is not. First it is a study in the book. Then it is a study with

people of what exists in two party's minds (individuals business or nations) when first confronted. A real time saver in evaluating possible compatibility or not between the two for anyone. It works.

20. "Passion Of Dance" This is a narrative on progress, value and guidance for the dance inclined. It's informative and inspiring with its history and recent magnetism.

21. "Open That Door" to love. This book is comprehensively all about love. It's not a storybook. It clears up the differences of love that causes misunderstanding, suspicion and deception.

22. "Get The Spirit" This book describes controversial and somewhat intertwined conventional views of spirit, spirits and spirituality. This book untangles the "usual" views and presents a more perspective manner of living with these concepts of mind.

23. "Stories Of What They Couldn't Or Wouldn't Tell" Ages are from babies to 100 years; twenty four of them.

24. "Improving On Love And Relationships" This one is two books in one. Part one "Open That Door" is a psychology of love that enhances perspective to understand and adapt to a very popular, but deceiving, repressed and ignored emotion; love. Part two covers "Relationships For All" which elaborates on origination, different types, significance, deceptions, desires, experiences, communication, possibilities, future and guidance of relationships. It's comprehensive and also derived from a lifetime of relationship experiences and serious study.

NOTES

NOTES

NOTES

NOTES

www.ingramcontent.com/pod-product-compliance
Lightning Source LLC
Chambersburg PA
CBHW020859310526
45786CB00018B/402